Just Get Dressed

Why you have nothing to wear... and what to do about it

Samantha Lee Harman

Hot Off the Press Ltd

For Irene, Julie, Charlotte, Beth, and Steph. And all the other women who made me, who shaped this book, who came before us, and who will come next.

Contents

Author's Note

The context of this book – 2026

It is a lie that you can't have style and substance. It's a fabrication created and upheld by those who benefit from patriarchy, a system that demands women's submission so it can continue selling us products, focusing our attention on what we don't need, instead of what we should have – power.

There is a version of you that you'll never meet. One who feels so at home in her skin, so beloved by her body, so in touch with the collective universal life-force, and so certain that women rise when we work together, that she actually embodies it all.

Patriarchy told you that to care about your appearance was stupid, yet it also told you that if you don't care, you are useless and unattractive.

And unattractiveness is far worse than stupidity.

It created infantilising beauty standards and pedestalled an impossible body type, because it knew that self-possessed women who accept themselves completely are the most powerful force on the planet. Patriarchy needed you to forget this for the sake of its survival.

It told you that dressing in a way that feels joyful is "too much" because women who feel amazing can and will do anything.

And women who can do anything are the stuff of nightmares for a system that relies on their submission.

This book is a refusal to submit.

This book is the result of growing sick and tired of a system that would rather be led by a law-breaking, evil, and incompetent man than accept an exceptional woman.

In reading this book, you will butt up against your own internalisation of patriarchy. You will feel a contraction every time I swear. You may wince when I say the thing we are not supposed to say. I want you to continue reading anyway, without self-judgement. This is the healing work, the necessary work, the reason this book has found you.

And whilst my note is here at the outset – so there can be no confusion as to what this book is really about (because it's never about the clothes) – you'll get much more from it when you come back at the end.

In case you're woefully unaware – or wilfully distracted – the era of being the kind of woman who refuses to do this work is well and truly over.

You are about to turn the page and get stuck in because you are committing to being the woman who no longer has her wardrobe weaponised against her, and instead, turns her wardrobe into a weapon against the patriarchy.

There is nothing the patriarchy fears more than a woman who wears whatever the fuck she likes, says what she likes and, importantly, likes herself.

She is the revolution.

Preface: The Safety Blanket

'You'll probably wear that black dress again,' sneered a friend as we discussed our outfits for an event. My other friends laughed. I felt the hot wave of shame wash over me, starting in my cheeks and working its way down to the areas of my body I barely acknowledge. I didn't have the vocabulary or the capacity to explain in that moment what my trusty black dress symbolised.

It meant safety.

I wore it because most of the time, I felt so uncomfortable in my own skin, it was like I was on fire.

Ever since I was about four years-old and was told the way I looked was "wrong" I'd been living with the constant, dull nagging of not-*enough*ness.

Like I'm *a lot*; but only in the *worst* ways. A lot of belly, a lot of thighs.

I remember being around eight years-old and looking at my thigh spread out across the car seat and feeling repulsed. Not because *I'd* decided there was something wrong with my body – society had.

That feeling of repulsion followed me around. It was zipped up against me inside all the clothes I wore, even that black dress. In the back of my mind, always, was the voice that said: 'You need to lose weight.'

I found myself justifying a slice of cake, or buying clothes two sizes too small as inspiration. But what did I expect when, as a child, I walked into shops to see beautiful Jessica Simpson splashed across magazines labelled "Jumbo Jessica"?[1]

Fast-forward to my twenties, and my black dress was the only thing in my wardrobe that made me feel just invisible enough to be seen. Yes, my wardrobe was full of other clothes. But most of them were "one day" fantasies; things I'd bought to slim into. They were snaffled in late-night emotionally-fragile moments when I dreamed of being anyone other than me. Or a me that was so different from this one, she always felt out of reach.

Most of the times when we'd go out, I had to psyche myself up to even get ready.

I spent loads of time on my hair so hopefully, maybe, it might distract from the belly I'd been trying my entire life to get away from.

I wore that dress because when we went shopping, there would be loads of stuff for my friends and nothing for me (except accessories, because as any woman who's ever struggled with her body will know, a handbag will always fit! hahafuckingha!)

My friends could pick up whatever took their fancy and I was left with a selection of cold-shoulder tops and empire waist dresses that looked more like something my Aunty Carol would wear to Benidorm than a 24-year-old would wear to the club.

That black dress was a safety blanket.

---

1. Sloss, M. (2022) *20 times women were Body-Shamed by the Media.* https://www.buzzfeed.com/morgansloss1/female-celebrities-body-shamed-by-media.

Introduction

Once you've read this book, or if you've come across me online as The Style Editor (a name that combines my background as a newspaper editor with my work in wardrobes), you might forget this story.

You might think, 'She's so confident. She wears such bright colours. I saw her on stage once and she was cracking jokes and flicking her hair with the confidence of a contestant on *Ru Paul's Drag Race*.'

...*she* only does all those things because she was once the girl in the black safety blanket.

That girl knows what it's like to never truly feel relaxed, alone or in public, because she's always fighting herself.

She knows what it's like to have a wardrobe full of "one day" clothes and still default to the same tired dress because it's either that, or she doesn't go to the party.

Her friends say they want her at the party. And she wants to believe them. She wants to believe it's because they enjoy her company. After all, she's spent a lifetime perfecting wit, charm, and humour as a deflection against the bullying and snide remarks. But deep down she fears the reason they want her at the party is because it makes them feel better. She's a court jester – there for entertainment, not emotional connection. Because when they're having a moment of self-doubt about their outfits, at least they're not the poor size-18 girl wearing that tired old black dress.

This book is for every woman who's had a black safety dress, and maybe still lives inside one.

It's for every woman who's ever stood in front of her wardrobe in panic, clothes discarded all over the floor, five minutes before leaving the house, tears of frustration in her eyes as she thinks, 'I'm such a fucking ugly fat potato.'

It's for every woman who's been spoken over by a man who knows about one per cent of what she does, but she doesn't feel confident enough to speak up.

It's for the women who put up with shitty behaviour in relationships because deep down they don't feel like they deserve any better.

It's for every woman who got sucked into "needing" the latest beauty treatment and realising the only thing that's losing pounds is her bank account.

It's for every woman who's found herself on the end of a nasty comment from her mother, her friend, or a stranger, that has limited what she wears, says, or does.

It's for the women who have this little voice in the back of their heads constantly saying, 'You've got to lose weight/you can't wear that/you can't do that/you're an imposter.'

It's for every woman who has a wardrobe full of clothes… and nothing to wear. Because "I have nothing to wear" has *nothing* to do with clothes.

Your wardrobe is the physical manifestation of your beliefs. With just a quick peek inside, I can garner a lot of information about the way you see yourself. Your hopes, dreams, fears, goals, the person you hope to become and the person you hope to never be. The parts of you that are hidden (perhaps even from yourself) and the parts of you not yet fully embraced.

And that's what makes this book different from anything else about the concept of "style" you might have read before.

This is not a paint-by-numbers, wear-these-specific-items book.

It's not a book that gives you a generic checklist of the things you "must have" in your wardrobe, as if *you're* generic and not a multi-faceted, complex, and sometimes contradictory human being.

It's not a book that assumes you're a total dummy who knows nothing about style or fashion, or yourself. It's a *work*book. And it's not really about clothes.

Haven't you ever wondered why you've got a wardrobe stuffed with them and yet still, you never feel quite at home in your outfits? Why, despite all the money spent and all the hours wasted, you still have nothing to wear?

Your wardrobe is not the cause – it is a symptom. Which is why this book isn't about what's hanging inside your wardrobe, but what it represents.

It's only fair that from the outset, I make two things clear.

One: I will not tell you what to wear.

This book does not contain outfit ideas, or rules, or colour palettes. There are many other books out there covering these principles. You can tie yourself up in knots about what the lauded author of that famous style book said you *should* and *shouldn't* wear if you want to. But to do so would be to completely miss the point of what's contained in the upcoming pages.

Whenever clients ask me, 'Does this look OK?' I tell them they are asking the wrong question.

The real question is – why are you asking someone else what you should wear? Why are you outsourcing your permission? The answer is not as simple as a sentence, but within these pages, I hope to help you find it.

Two: this book will not change your life.

This book alone has as much chance of changing your life as all the new bags, shoes, clothing, skincare, and other books you bought under the promise to yourself that they would change your life, too. You never wear them, never use them, never read them – and therefore, no magic result.

Without your commitment to turning each page of this book and doing the work I will ask of you along the way, it is just a collection of pages, bound together by glue and string. It's an inanimate object with no more use than as a doorstop or a balancing shelf for your laptop when you're on Teams calls.

Words alone printed on a page, inside a book you barely open, tucked on a shelf or plonked beside your bed for the next six months, will not change your life.

You will change your life.

This *work*book does not work unless you do. I'm passing you the tools, but I'm trusting you to carry out the process. And I'm telling you this now, so if you're not the kind of person willing to do the work, you can shut this book and shut me up along with it, and get on with your life.

Best wishes. No hard feelings.[1]

Still here? Great. Let's go.

Outsourcing your style is outsourcing your power and it shows up *everywhere* – not just your wardrobe.

It's the way you bite your tongue about behaviour that erodes your relationships with certain people. It's there when you say "sure" to your boss about taking on yet more work, even though you're not being paid nearly enough for this shit. It's why you say "fine thanks" when the waiter comes over to ask about your meal and you can barely chew through the cremated chicken. It's how you wedge in "just" and "sorry" after every other word even though you're simply communicating what needs to be done. It's why you struggle on with the work and the household tasks and the childcare without thinking help might be available, because the female condition equals martyrdom. It's why, when someone asks what you do, you go, 'Erm, I kind of do this little, like, thing, it's no big deal.'

It's all the undercharging, overdelivering, putting everyone else first, exhausting fucking nonsense you put up with that makes you want to scream.

But you don't scream.

You internalise all the rage, let your organs and autoimmune system suffer, and carry on putting up with sub-par treatment, experiences, and style because you do not believe you have permission for anything else.

---

1. Extremely hard feelings. I take this very personally and I am plotting petty revenge.

And *that's* why "What's new at [popular store]" or "5 ways to wear a turtleneck" or "the trends you need to know this season" are fun and all, but… they're not changing anything.

You've ended up with a digital mountain of "how to style" posts saved in your Instagram, no intention of ever implementing them, and a wardrobe full of stuff you don't wear.

You're here because you're sick and tired and you've been searching for answers.

The bad news is – I don't have them. The good news is – *you do.*

Just Get Dressed is about uncovering the thing that's really missing from your wardrobe – *you.*

Not a surface-level version of who the world says you should be.

The you hidden beneath layers of life fabric.

The you who wouldn't get to the point of wanting to scream FUCK OFF FUCK OFF FUCK OFFFFFF to the world because she's confident expressing herself and she has not-to-be-fucked-with-in-the-first-place energy.

Why I wrote this book

I know you're here begrudgingly. All sorts of negatives are running through your head right now.

I shouldn't need help with this

This is going to cost time I don't have.

I hate that this matters.

It's ridiculous that I'm a grown up and I'm here reading a book about style. Who fucking cares how I dress?!

My advice? Feel it all.

Write out all your objections. Process your feelings. Most of my clients start exactly where you are now, scrolling LinkedIn, feeling triggered as fuck by some of the things I'm saying. Not wanting to admit they feel this way, they continuously put up with the struggle, until some shitty moment forces them to address the mess they've been hiding inside their wardrobes.

'I hate that I need help with this,' a new client said to me the other day. Me too.

When I think about the gender disparities in how we are "supposed" to dress, how women specifically are judged on what we wear, on the non-standardised sizing designed to make us hate our bodies, the way our wardrobes are wrapped up in patriarchy, the privilege that comes with being able to say, 'I don't care what I wear'…

It makes me mad as hell. So mad, in fact, that I wrote a whole book about it.

It *does* matter, which is **precisely why we should be getting style support.**

You can't opt out of style. You can have *bad* style (ethically, or style that doesn't reflect you) but you can't opt out altogether. *Because you wear clothes.*

Resisting support keeps you stuck in the cycle of feeling frustrated, overwhelmed, and playing into the status quo.

This isn't a niche problem. You are not a freak, a weirdo, or whatever other nonsense you're telling yourself. It's very common and it impacts our money and power. I work with women at every stage – from returning to corporate after maternity leave to CEOs hitting seven figures – and not a single one of them is unaffected by style struggles.

This is why the problem is not something that can be fixed by buying a whole load of new clothes on our own. You *know* this. If that was the solve, you wouldn't be here, reading this book. You wouldn't have an overstuffed wardrobe, and you wouldn't have clothes shoved in the boot of your car you've been meaning to take to the charity shop for the last six months.

The reason you've got decision paralysis about what to wear has nothing to do with the clothes. It's because you're always trying to make the correct decision based not on what you *want* to wear, but on what you think the world will tolerate.

You're caught between "don't attract attention" and "attention is currency." Between "fit in" and "fuck the old guard." Between "be a good girl" and "be the rebel."

Knowing so many women are holding off from fulfilling their potential keeps me awake at night. It's the reason I am at my keyboard at 4am writing this.

The biggest issue with your wardrobe isn't what's in it. It's that you have no power over it.

There is always someone else who knows more than you, right? An Instagram stylist dictating what you should wear (never mind her "expertise" boils down to a one-day training course), whose rules keep you small.

This book is here to give your power back. Or rather, to help you rediscover it.

How to use this book

I'm not selling instant wardrobe joy. I struggled for years. Crying in changing rooms? Tick. Being body shamed? Tick. Being turned down for jobs because I wasn't the "correct aesthetic"? YUP.

I thought style was unavailable to me. Then one day, the veil lifted and I realised: I get to give myself permission. Out go all the rules I grew up believing. Now, I genuinely wear what I love. I use my wardrobe as a strategic and energetic tool for making money, and I refuse to waste another moment of my one precious, magical life believing I can't wear *that* because I've got a belly.

This isn't a "click your heels together three times and you'll suddenly feel stylish too" situation. The work *takes work*. And this book is going to guide you through it.

Firstly we'll uncover why you have nothing to wear – then we'll look at what to do about it.

I'm going to guide you through the process I use with clients – incredible women like you. And just like you, they couldn't see their incredibleness at the start, either. Now they're running great businesses, bagging promotions, writing books, and leading panels. If the idea of doing just one of those things excites you, this book is going to get you to dream and think big. Here's how we'll do it:

- We'll discover where "the rules" came from and why you're being told to compare your lovely natural body to pieces of fruit.
- We can't create new wardrobe habits without uncovering and understanding our current ones, so one of the first actions is the Outfit Diary.

- Then we're going to map out your big goals and vision (no downplaying or making do on my watch).
- We'll get stuck into your wardrobe and get rid of the things that aren't working.
- Once you're ready, we'll learn how to shop like professionals, challenge your self-sabotage (because that bitch will crop up), and unlock all the potential of your wardrobe.

Here's the big secret about style: the definition given to you by fashion magazines is made up. It's a marketing ploy. It's all about women playing by "the rules" and looking for permission about what to wear. They dictate what's hot and what's not based on whims. The whole industry keeps us in a holding pattern – always searching but never finding what we're looking for. It's like trying to grab air (which, if we continue buying too many clothes in our search for style, we'll soon be running out of).

Real style is not decked in designer, it's mixing pieces, textures, eras, and aesthetics to create something uniquely you. *You* get to define what style means for yourself.

This is why I refuse to normalise your style struggles. Normalising style struggles suits the status quo. If it's normal for women to spend lifetimes struggling with their image, wrestling with their wardrobes, and thinking "one day" when we have a finite number of days left, it means we don't have the capacity to change what really needs changing in the world.

The reason you have nothing to wear is about you – but it's also much bigger than you. It's the invisible Style Tax you pay because of patriarchal gender constructs. It's about the women who came before you and those who come next.

This book will ask you questions about your style you've likely never been asked before. You'll uncover the link between what you wear, how you feel, who benefits from that, and how you miss out.

This isn't the kind of book you just read, or worse – flick through and put on the bookshelf. It's a book you use. If you tag me in a story with the awesome cover then I find out you're using it for the aesthetics, not the gold inside? Girl... I'll be round your house faster than you can say OOTD.

The best books I have ever read make me want to act. They fill my mind with ideas and inspiration and most importantly, the impetus to *do something*. And I hope I have written a book like that for you. It's a metaphorical shake of the shoulders for every woman who's currently downplaying, hiding, and not living her full potential. The women who are so fucking talented and beautiful but have been caged by lies because holy shit, things would change if they were unleashed. One of those women is *you*.

Personal style is available to you, because, well, it's personal. This book is going to put the *you* back into your wardrobe.

First, we burn the rulebook. Then, we get to work. Ready?

Part One
Why You Have Nothing to Wear

Just get dressed.

If only it were that simple.

You've got clothes, right? You don't *have* to be naked. So why does it feel like you have nothing to wear?

It's the weather. It's how your day is filled with different scenarios that require different things from your clothes. It's that you're still carrying a little extra holiday weight and you've got to punish yourself into losing it. Your one good top is in the wash – and a whole load of other surface-level style struggles.Except, it's not any of those things.

If we're going to create a wardrobe that *actually* works for you, we need to understand why it currently doesn't. And I don't mean because you're missing a decent pair of jeans and the right shoes. I mean the deep-seated beliefs dictating what's in your drawers and the cultural normalisation of women having "nothing to wear."

You have nothing to wear because that suits society. It's not an issue with clothes – it's a feminist matter.

The more time, resource, and effort you spend on trying to figure out this problem on your own, or convincing yourself it's not a problem – the less time, resource, and effort you have to put towards the things that really matter.

I call the emotional, mental, and financial limits that impact your wardrobe the Style Tax – and this book is about reducing your bill. If you identify as or have been raised female, there will be obvious costs, systemic and hidden, associated with your identity. In this book, we'll dissect these in detail so you can recognise them and reduce them.

There are stylists who will tell you to buy 10 dresses and send you on your way. And some women are perfectly happy with that. It's a way of saying you did the work and you have style, when what you've actually done is… buy 10 new dresses.

I am not interested in you having 10 new dresses. I am interested in you having 10 new mindset perspectives that will change the way you dress forever and turn your wardrobe from out-of-control entity to money-making tool. Throughout this book there are lots of questions designed to help you achieve this.

Chapter 1

Dressed in Nuance

Dressing is not frivolous. It's a feminist act. You are allowed to be multifaceted.

Can you really enjoy dressing up and be feminist?

Can you really like funky earrings and be intelligent?

Can you have a pair of Louboutins on your vision board *and* be tapped into what's going on in the world?

I bet those questions (or variations) were running through your head when you picked up this book.

Women are taught that being multifaceted is failing.

You won't be taken seriously if you admit you want to look and feel stylish, will you?

You may have wondered what people would say if they knew you cared enough about style to read a book about it. You may be reading this under the cloak of darkness, underneath your duvet with the light from your phone, or covertly placed inside another book on the train, for fear of judgement. Maybe you bought it years ago but are only just now picking it up, because for ages you've been thinking, 'I get dressed every day, I don't need help with this!'

Whatever the reason you picked up a book about having nothing to wear and what to do about it, chances are the question, 'But can I enjoy dressing up and be feminist?' has crossed your mind. Rather than labelling you silly or frivolous, I'd say that your being here demonstrates your intelligence.

And yes, of course I am going to say picking up my book is a smart move, because I'm an Aries with an ego problem, and I self-published, but that aside – you already know this is no ordinary style book. You know the intention is to make you a smarter shopper, a more considerate dresser, and a better leader.

If you were silly or frivolous, you wouldn't be here. You'd still be caught up in the same old cycle of having nothing to wear, buying things you won't put on, and pretending not to be part of fashion's toxic climate-killing problem.

We live in a society that has normalised women being in a state of perpetual style struggle. The bigger the struggle, the smaller our resolve for solving the problems that truly matter.

There is a difference between getting dressed because you can't be naked and getting dressed to create the life you want. And when it comes to getting dressed in any capacity, there's a whole lot of gaslighting going on, all with the sole intention of making you buy stuff, but then not letting you talk about the stuff, so you end up with an insurmountable amount of stuff and no room in your brain for other stuff.

Don't you dare shine too brightly

We see time and time again how women who dare to shine too brightly, or who are perceived as too much, are punished. Women who dare to show more than one part of their personalities, or who dare to be unapologetically sexy when their body doesn't conform to narrow beauty standards, are ridiculed, mocked, and passed over.

Multimillionaire and feminist icon Tori Dunlap lost more than 40,000 Instagram followers when she dared post a photo of herself in a bikini. She was told by people who'd literally profited from her financial expertise by way of free content in the form of podcasts, daily social media posts, and courses, that they could no longer take her seriously.

Musician Chappell Roan received backlash when she spoke out about people shouting at her or touching her in the street because they think they have a right to her, because she's famous.

Women don't get to be or have both. They don't get the right to put their art into the world *and* also have privacy. They don't get to be wildly rich *and* exist free from commentary about their looks. They don't get to wear whatever the fuck they want *and* get the corner office.

And it's not just in public. A friend of mine was told her contract to deliver training for a company was no longer going ahead because she was too outspoken online. Ya know, just voicing some stuff about her lived experience of sexism, but it's inappropriate.

The difference in how we are judged, treated and what is expected of us as women is very much playing out inside your closet. How?

You can't opt out of clothing

You are part of the fashion industry by virtue of the fact you wear clothes. There is no opting out of consumerism when you live in a culture, as I assume you do, that makes it illegal to be naked in public. Not to mention that here in the UK, your bits are going to turn blue pretty quick without them.

Aside from the legal and health implications of not wearing clothes, emerging changes in how we work, live, and interact with one another mean that unless you want to go live in a cave and never speak to another human being ever again (tempting, I know) – saying "no thanks" to fashion is not really an option.

It's all very well to throw our hands in the air exasperated and be all 'for god's sake, get over it! It's no big deal!' But that would be to dismiss an industry worth trillions of dollars, all the people who work in it, the psychological impact of what we wear, and the way it's shaped your relationship with yourself.

It's virtually impossible to stay offline (not sure I could do it, even if I was living in that cave) and the first thing a date will do is look us up on social media. Seventy per cent of employers screen candidates based on their digital footprint. Without social media, I would not have built the business or the audience to allow me to write this book. And without social media, you likely wouldn't be reading it.

We form a first impression of someone within seconds (some researchers think it's as fast as one-tenth of a second[1]). And what do we use to assess if we assimilate with someone and decide if their book might be for us?

What they're wearing.

The tools at our disposal might be modern, but assimilation and

---

1. Willis, J., & Todorov, A. (2006). First Impressions: Making Up Your Mind After a 100-Ms Exposure to a Face. *Psychological Science*, *17*(7), 592–598. https://doi.org/10.1111/j.1467-9280.2006.01750.x

ritual through clothing is not. Archaeological evidence, such as perforated Nassarius shells found at Blombos Cave in South Africa, suggests humans were stringing and wearing shells as beads at least 75,000 years ago.

So to act like we can just opt out of the clothing conversation is not a flex. It reeks of defence, privilege, and ego. Most recently I've come to realise it's a convenient way of shutting women down. We tell women they're vain, selfish, and silly for caring about style. We act like it's anti-feminist while wearing a "feminist" slogan T-shirt made in a sweatshop by a 12-year-old girl.

Learning about style is, in fact, the *feminist* thing to do. Garment workers are predominantly female. Fashion consumers are predominantly female. The majority of household purchasing decisions are made by women and they are the majority target of fashion and beauty advertising. Surely it would be better to educate ourselves on who made our clothes, where they come from, how they're being used against us and, importantly, how we can use them, than to shame one another for the way we relate to them?

In any other context, learning is encouraged. When people say they're learning about the clothes they put on their backs? *SELFISHHH!!* Isn't that interesting? I've been wondering lately if that's because clothing is seen as inherently female and what we're saying about the feminine is that it equals weakness.

I've seen the same people who shame those working on their style praise those investing in a new website – like one is a serious business tool, but not the other.

Once you educate yourself on what you're wearing, you understand that the selfish behaviour is accumulating low-cost clothes then dumping them to charity (not that most of it goes there, as you'll learn) after one wear because it didn't fit right or look right or wasn't actually what you wanted; you just bought it because it was cheap.

When retailers are selling clothes for £2.99, the buyer has no idea of the planetary and human costs. Shoppers view products as disposable, as temporary, as fleeting as (and less expensive than) their morning cup of coffee.

There will always be a need for affordable clothing. But I don't believe those who have the real and pressing need for affordable clothing are the ones fuelling our overconsumption. If someone desperately needs a new outfit, I don't believe they're on TikTok shop, adding £200 of clothes to their basket after a shitty day at work, sipping on a prosecco whilst watching *Friends* reruns.

Our reliance on new clothes stems from much deeper issues than having "nothing to wear."

"Nothing to wear" is not literal

There are plenty of clothes in our closets. "Nothing to wear" is shorthand for "I don't know who I'm supposed to be, I don't know how to mould myself into the specific thing the world wants me to be at this very moment."

It's why you've saved so many of those capsule wardrobe checklists and you've tried it once or twice but still feel stifled.

The second reason why this clothing conversation is very much about gender? Clothing is a tool that a specific type of man has been using for decades to get ahead and stay there.

Did you know that in traditional business dress codes, there is a whole other level where it's just things for people who identify as male? Of course, no one is *saying* women can't be in charge of the boardroom, but it shows that when these dress codes were laid out, the idea of a woman in that seat was so unimaginable they didn't even bother coming up with any guidance about what she should wear.

As archaic as that sounds, and as much as we like to believe things have moved on, the actual bread-and-butter of dress codes has not.

One study found that men spend more on clothing than women, yet women shop more.[2] This suggests that whilst women may use shopping for recreation and even emotional comfort, men have a higher sense of self-esteem and are happier to spend more on one item than women are.

I've seen this many times over with clients. One was in management earning well over six-figures. She'd seen a designer jacket she loved, and despite being able to afford it she decided to buy several high-street versions. None of the high-street versions were any good. So she bought another. Five unsuitable jackets and the best part of £500 later – not to mention all that time she spent searching online, purchasing, and returning – she could have bought the designer jacket she really wanted.

Time saved, probably money saved, and she'd have felt more like a leader. But the money in my client's bank account didn't make any difference when the stories in her head were all about unworthiness.

---

2. Davis, J. (2018) 'Apparently, men spend more on clothes than women do,' *Harper's BAZAAR*, 22 February. https://www.harpersbazaar.com/uk/fashion/a18207166/apparently-men-spend-more-on-clothes-than-women-do/

The systems converging in your closet

You are a multi-faceted human being, living in a world of contradictions, where different systems co-exist and converge in your closet.

Sometimes women come to work with me under a self-inflicted pressure that they're supposed to find one specific style and stick to it. It's like they're standing in front of a row of boxes and they think they're supposed to find the one they fit neatly into with the lid closed. They think they are the problem; that style is a conundrum to solve, not a giant, joyful experiment in self-expression.

So what if rather than the women, it's the boxes that are the problem? What if you don't have to be either/or? You can be both. You can be all.

It's OK if the answer to some of the questions in this book – or elsewhere in your life – is "I don't know yet."

It's OK if the answer is "I don't know, ever."

It's OK if you select multiple answers, not one.

Nuance has checked out of conversation in the digital age. You're not allowed to live in the grey area. But the grey area is all that truly exists. It's OK if you don't fit neatly into one style box; I certainly don't.

You can be sexy one day (however you define it), demure the next, in classics and masculine energy tomorrow, floaty and floral on Friday. The point of style isn't to commit to one specific, rigid template for "how to dress" and fill your wardrobe with only things that relate to that particular aesthetic. The point of style is that your wardrobe encapsulates you. *All of you.*

Good style is not following trends or looking like a fashion plate. It's not following a paint-by-numbers guide to building an outfit. It's the skill of taking various elements of who you are and blending them together to create something unique.

Style is not black and white, one-dimensional. It's nuanced, multi-faceted, and multi-coloured. If you can learn how to exist in, and dress for, the nuance – that's where the magic is. But in order to find your special brand of nuance, we need to go back in time and unlearn some of the stories currently playing in your style…

Your style assessment

This set of prompts will help you define your style, the stories in your wardrobe and, importantly, how you'd like to approach the work in this book.

I encourage you to grab a pen and paper and treat this as a journaling-style exercise, rather than just doing it in your head. When we write, we think differently and more deeply. We gain new insights into ourselves.

- Which is your favourite season for dressing? Why?
- Do you notice any differences in your behaviour when it comes to dressing in, shopping for, or planning your outfits for the season, depending on if you love it or hate it?
- Patterns and prints – which do you like? Which would you never wear? Or maybe you hate them altogether?
- Are there any styles or types of clothing you've never tried but would?
- Are there any styles of clothing you'd love to wear in an

ideal world, but don't? What does "an ideal world" mean in this context?

- Jewellery and accessories – yes or no? Big and bold, or small and dainty?
- Are you a gold or silver girl? Or maybe both? Or maybe neither?
- If you could live in any era of style, which would it be, and why?
- If you had a celebrity style icon, or several style icons, who would they be, and why?
- If you had to trade wardrobes with someone, who would it be and why?
- Is there anyone who you would *hate* to swap wardrobes with? Why?
- What are your current sources of style inspiration?
- What is the most worn item in your wardrobe? Why?
- Why did you buy this book?
- What do you hope to learn, discover, or change by being here?

Take all of the answers to those questions, everything you *think* you know about your style, and ask…

- Is this really true?
- Is it true that I'd never wear [certain style], or is there an underlying belief or story about this?
- How would I cope if I had to trade wardrobes with the person whose style I hate?
- How much of this would be what I'd choose of my own volition, and what is the result of social constructs?

Chapter 2

You're Not Dressing in a Silo

Your clothing choices are not just about what to wear. You're surrounded by ghosts, expectations, and inherited rules in a world that has always tried to dictate how you should appear.

You are never alone when you get dressed.

Standing in front of the wardrobe, as soon as the question "what should I wear?" arises, about 500 simultaneous conversations start happening in your head.

I wore that last time...

Steve from accounts made that gross comment...

The buttons do up weirdly on that...

I never got around to having this cleaned, that makes me bad...

It's a waste if I wear this outfit on a nothing day...

If I wore this, even though I love it, people might think it's a bit much...

I saw a woman wear something similar to this on LinkedIn and it attracted negative comments...

It's me, I'M THE PROBLEM.

The ghosts in your wardrobe

It's not that you have nothing to wear. It isn't *you* at all. It's all the other people standing in the room with you as you get dressed. I don't mean *literally standing in the room* – I'm guessing you aren't a queen from the Regency period and you don't have a team of dressers.

I mean your mother and her body dysmorphic diet patterns, the way she was always looking in the mirror and pinching at her non-existent wobbly bits. That teacher from Year 5 who called you chubby and wouldn't let you be on the netball team even though you were really good at netball (true story). The first boyfriend who cheated on you, the old boss who used to stare at your boobs instead of paying attention to your brains, the random strangers on social media who make mean, disparaging comments and use the internet as an emotional punchbag rather than going to therapy.

When you get dressed, you're doing it against the backdrop of the day's political climate and social fabrics, the ghostly memories of all the people who've ever commented on your appearance or dress sense, or even your capabilities.

You're dressing among the limiting beliefs to which you aren't cognisant... the generational patterns and stories we pass down through the ages... the media and the constant pressure to look better and be better, but within goalposts that are always moving... The potential attraction of visibility on social media – a relatively new concept in the grand scheme of things... The impending climate crisis, not helped at all by how we see clothes as more transient than a cup of coffee...

You are never alone in your wardrobe. Sorry if that sounds spooky.

Whether it's a passing remark someone made when you were 17, a nasty comment about a woman you saw on LinkedIn today, or media rhetoric about what a celebrity wore, we can't always shut the door or switch off the phone when these things are already imprinted in our brains.

Every negative comment or sarcastic remark is confirming your belief that you are a terrible, awful, failure with no fashion sense. You unconsciously weigh up the kind of reaction you'll get to your new outfit in a world that allows its media to use language like "she flaunted her legs" because a woman dared to wear a skirt. You're not just thinking about whether *you* like this top, but will your mum, who's always banging on about your short neck, like it on you too? And if you choose this dress for your business meeting, will Brian take you seriously, or will you feel his eyes on your boobs?

I want you to consider how when you get dressed, it's not happening in isolation. Your clothing choices – whether conscious or not – are made in the context of the society in which you live. There are literal laws and regulations and guidelines outlining what is and isn't acceptable on the street and in your office. There are different cultural norms and expectations. And there are also lots of unspoken expectations, the parameters for which are constantly changing, that are floating around the room every time you put on clothes.

You may have come to this book simply wanting to know how to save a bit of time in the mornings not stressing about what to wear. But having nothing to wear, or being confused about what to wear to a specific event, are as much about the things going on around you as they are about what's in your wardrobe.

The good news is, once you understand this, you are able to use your clothes to change the context. You can make deliberate choices about what to wear and communicate with those around you why you've made those choices, not only improving your own personal brand, visibility, and impact, but theirs, too.

So if you aren't wearing clothes, what are you wearing?

You're wearing your grandma's stories

Since we absorb so much from the women who raise us, we are shaped in part by their views, beliefs and experiences. A rule about what to wear passed down from your grandmother was passed down by hers, meaning you are dressing today in stories dating back to the Victorian era. Think how much has changed about society, technology and women's rights since then. Yet we still carry the baggage.

As an innocuous example: blue and green should never be seen. It's thought this phrase derives from seafarers, warning that fishermen should not paint the hulls of their boats green because they would be hard to distinguish from the colour of the sea. A literal old wives' tale about fishermen is stopping you from styling your green top and blue skirt together.

Aside from stories passed down through the ages, stored trauma is alive and well in your style choices. Epigenetics is a scientific field with growing research to suggest that experiences are passed down through generations. This concept, known as intergenerational transmission of trauma effects, was first recognised in studies of survivors of the Dutch famine in the Second World War and Holocaust survivors.

Scientists found that traumatic events can influence our genes. They don't change our DNA, but they guide which genes are activated. Survivors of childhood trauma or abuse appear to have children with increased risk of PTSD, anxiety, diabetes, and obesity.[1]

Considering that your mother came from an egg from your grandmother, who came from an egg from your great-grandmother, it's not unreasonable to surmise that some of the things you're experiencing now started hundreds of years ago. Not all trauma is yours – it's inherited. You may have no logical explanation or reason for why certain things give you anxiety, why you have a distrust of certain events or feel unsafe in certain situations, or why you have physical symptoms – but the answer could be something that happened back in 1919 to your great-grandmother.

A study on mice, published in 2014, found that the trauma of a generation can impact the behaviour of descendants. The grandchildren of mice which had been exposed to electric shock when they smelled cherries were "highly fearful" of the smell of cherries. Scientists discovered that the DNA of the grandfather mouse's sperm had changed after he received the shock, and generations later, his descendants were wary when they smelled cherries.[2]

This realisation hit me like a brick when I was fortunate (if that is the correct term) to be invited to Buckingham Palace.

Being in Buckingham Palace was never on the list of things I thought I might one day do. But in the summer of 2018 I had won some big journalism awards and I got invited to meet the Queen. Trying to find a palace-appropriate outfit (add that to my

---

1. Wolynn, M. (2016) *It Didn't Start with You: How Inherited Family Trauma Shapes Who We Are and How to End the Cycle*.
2. Dias, B.G. and Ressler, K.J. (2013) 'Parental olfactory experience influences behavior and neural structure in subsequent generations,' *Nature Neuroscience*, 17(1), pp. 89–96. https://doi.org/10.1038/nn.3594.

styling CV) wasn't just about the clothes or the rules. It was about how, despite all the work and the accolades, I still felt like the girl from the council estate who *didn't belong here.*

I could hardly believe this resplendent, peaceful sanctuary existed in the middle of one of the busiest cities in the world. As I looked up, I noticed tower blocks on the skyline. The contrast could not be greater. It made me think about my grandad, who grew up in a tenement in the Gorbals in Glasgow. He was the descendent of Irish immigrants who came over in the famine. As a child, he sometimes had to eat coal. He'd been in Borstal, joined the army, and let's just say he had a few holidays at Her Majesty's pleasure.

Just two generations removed, I've been to university, became the first female editor of the newspaper I worked for in 160 years (and one of the few firsts in the history of UK newspapers), created a six-figure business, and written a book. I know that's because my parents and grandparents worked hard to show me that life existed beyond the struggle of where you're born, but the point is – I did not do those things without it.

Jock died when I was five, but I still remember his thick Glaswegian accent (I was barely able to understand a word he said), his bristly moustache, and his Bovril-stained vest. I did not know him all that well, but I do feel how his lived trauma, and those of his ancestors, have imprinted on me. And this is why we cannot go forward into the wardrobe before we go back into the past. We barely acknowledge this, but as a first-in-generations kind of woman doing things our ancestors could not, we are unpicking the threads of their experiences as we navigate our own.

You exist right there by that lake – suspended in limbo between the *haves* and *the struggle*. Not feeling like you really belong here at the palace, but also like you can never go back to the place you once called home. Angry at the centuries-old systems that oppressed your people, and accepting the invitation anyway, because you feel like it makes you valid.

Your decisions about what to wear today did not take place today. They started years ago with the people who made you and raised you. Ask yourself: what were the experiences they navigated, and how might they be impacting me in the present?

Just Get Dressed: End of chapter task

Who's in the room with you when you get dressed?

Close your eyes and imagine standing in front of the doors of a huge closet. Inside are all your dream outfits, things you'd love to wear. Your tummy is leaping as you stand in anticipation and excitement.

Everything is bathed in a rich golden light.

You grab both handles of the heavy doors and swing them open to select an outfit. In front of you is the thing you would wear if you felt no pressure or sense of obligation, if you had never heard any rules, if you had not been conditioned to be a good girl.

Suddenly the light fades to grey and the outfit begins to disintegrate. And standing to your shoulder you notice a figure with a wand who cast the spell to make this happen.

- Who is this figure? What are they saying?
- What memory do they come from?
- What do you need to tell them?
- What do you need to take from this?

Just Get Dressed

We are working towards deliberate choices and the power they hold. Once you understand this, you are able to use your clothes to change the context.

Chapter 3

The Mother of All Subjects

Your mother is in your wardrobe whether you like it or not.

Whether you completely reject everything she stood for, or you're living in her shadow, your mother is hanging out amongst the dresses in your closet.

I have chosen to write this as a separate chapter, so if the topic feels too traumatic, or there are some dark corners of your inner mind wardrobe you'd rather not shine a light on right now, you can skip right by.

Carrie Bradshaw once said: "The most exciting, challenging and significant relationship of all is the one you have with yourself."

In my experience, having worked with hundreds of women, your relationship with yourself becomes the one it needs to become, once you have dissected your relationship (or lack thereof) with your mother.

Of course, I am basing this on people who identify as female, but if you are male or male-identifying, non-binary, or identify in another way, you may find it helpful to conduct this exercise with any figure you consider to be the main guardian or parent you had as a child.

Your mother is supposed to be your first role model, the one who should demonstrate unconditional love. She probably taught you a lot about style – whether it was a subject for which she had plenty of time, or absolutely none. She taught you what it meant to be a woman. Whether she was the epitome of martyrdom, sacrificing herself then growing increasingly resentful, or whether she valued material possessions above all, and you felt deprioritised in her pursuit of work, money, or men. Whether she was over-bearing, critical, more like a friend, never present, or a wonderful parent, she has influenced you in ways that perhaps you love, or hate.

People are doing the best with the information they have. Your mother is no exception. She has a mother, who had a mother, and all of them were a product of the environment in which they existed. And let's not forget the societal stigma, pressure, and unreachable standards placed on motherhood. Mothers are criticised regardless of the choices they make. It's a vital role for the continuation of the human race, but one steeped in burden and pressure. That said, the collective weight of motherhood does not absolve your individual mother for any behaviour that hurt you, and it does not negate your lived experience, either.

If you are someone who believes in life purpose, which I guess you are because you're here, then maybe healing the stories for the women in your lineage feels like an important part of your work.

Whether you are a parent yourself or not, try to remove your own experience of being or having a mother from this conversation. This isn't really between you and your mother; it's between *you* and *you*. You can't heal someone else's trauma. You can't force them to change. You can read this and get riled up and send your mother a message about all the ways you feel she's wronged you, but I promise it won't have the desired effect. Unless the desired effect is to hurt feelings, which I don't believe you want to do. And perhaps you do not have a mother; perhaps she is no longer with us or you are estranged.

I have written this chapter as a general summary, and I trust that you can approach it with the critical awareness that it's your work to uncover how these things have impacted you in your individual circumstance.

You are a good person and you understand your role here is not destruction, but healing. You can't do your mother's work for her, but you can work on your mother's trauma as it exists within you. And in turn, you're doing the work so your daughter doesn't have to.

No one gave your mother a manual on how to parent, or how to be a woman. She grew up in a time before community in the way we know it – no quickly WhatsApping a friend, or replying to Instagram stories. No online forums where she could exist under the relative safety of anonymity asking, 'Am I doing it right?' She was likely raised in a time before women were allowed to have financial freedom or a world-class education. She also has, or had, her own mother – and their relationship will likely have threads into yours.

You may have found you became her everything: your role was less daughter than it was therapist, coach, and confidante. Or maybe you became her nothing: she rejected the principle of motherhood and you haven't spoken in years. Even if you have an amicable relationship with your mother, perhaps you know it can only be that way as long as you comply with the unspoken rule of overlooking certain behaviours. Maybe you and your mum are the best of friends. The intention of this chapter is not to unpick the carefully cared-for threads of your relationship. It's to help you explore yourself.

Inside your wardrobe exists a version of your mother, whether true to the real one or an imagined version of what she could be, or all the parts of her you reject. You have to seek to understand the woman who made you, and the woman who made her, if you are going to fully understand yourself.

Just Get Dressed: End of chapter task

These questions will help you make sense of where your mother, or the main female role models in your life, are hanging out in your wardrobe. You don't have to complete this task if you feel triggered.

- What was your relationship with your mother like?
- What was her relationship with her mother?
- When you think about the women in your lineage, what's your overarching feeling? How much do you feel there is to overcome or heal?
- What was your mother's relationship with clothes?
- What was your mother's money story?

In answering these questions, what do you now understand about your relationship with your wardrobe?

Chapter 4

Your First Memory of Style

The beliefs sabotaging your wardrobe were formed in childhood and were never yours to begin with.

One of my first memories is standing on a stool, in my little knickers, wearing mum's shoes and sunglasses, singing *I'm Too Sexy* by Right Said Fred. I had no concept of "sexy" but I felt it. I believe this memory is tattooed into my brain because it was one of the last times I felt not just at home in my body, but like my body was a celebration.

And because I enjoyed celebrating my body through dance, my parents, who did not have much, worked hard to send me to dance lessons. Unfortunately, that meant for most of my childhood, every Saturday morning, I was facing the wall.

As I was soon to discover, there is a *right* way and a *wrong* way to dance. Dance is not self-expression, it turned out. It's a series of movements designed to stretch and contort the body for the judgement of other people.

I could never get it right.

I was too big. Too cumbersome. Too clumsy. Too heavy-footed. Too much to be considered a pretty little ballerina. I asked too many questions, which got me nicknamed Miss Contrary. So I was sent to the corner, to face the wall.

No matter how hard I tried, how long I practised after school, how much I thought about ballet in my sleep, how much I stopped myself from eating certain foods or memorised the Weight Watchers calorie book, it was never good enough. I'd twirl as fast as I could only to be screamed at, and sent to the corner once more.

Dance completely lost its joy for me. I dreaded it.

An activity I remembered loving, unencumbered by my apparent cumbersomeness, became a chore, a punishment, a terror. Every concert season, I'd stand stripped to my knickers in front of the woman who made our dance costumes. Lips pursed tightly around a cigarette, heaving as she spoke, she'd poke me in my belly and tell me how fat I was.

The little belly I used to enjoy became a source of shame. Enjoying your belly is a jarring concept for us today, because we live in a world that demonises them.

My dance teacher and the woman who made our costumes were responsible for their own behaviour. But they were also products of their environment.

Belly is a bad word

Good person? Cool. Work hard? Great. Got a talent? Wonderful… It's just, well… you've got a belly so regardless of any of that, you're incorrect. There was clearly a malfunction on the assembly line when they made you.

In 2000, Reebok released an advert depicting a man running away from a giant belly, played over with the soundtrack "belly's gonna get ya." I was around 10 when that advert came out. You can imagine what that did for my experience as "the fat kid" at school.

The presence of a belly is seen as a moral failing, and yet women need around nine per cent more body fat than men. Some fat is essential for your body to function. Yet you've spent a lifetime trying to get rid of this precious, life-saving resource.

In an article titled *How Rubenesque became a dirty word* for *The Telegraph*, Susie Orbach writes:

> "The relish of 17th-Century Flemish artist Peter Paul Rubens's lusciousness hurts the modern eye. We are discomfited by his notion of a female beauty that is so at odds with current tastes [...] despite some women's attempts to reclaim the Rubenesque body – and indeed despite women's struggles to be taken seriously whatever their size today – they remain a minority view. Our contemporary picture of femininity remains a narrow representation of form. We make unconscious judgements before we even know we are doing so. Our eyes are still trained to appreciate thin and slender bodies, while to be large continues to be derided, pitied, scorned, and depending on one's social location, to be discriminated against. Size has come to be regarded as something an individual can control. And variation, particularly of the ample sort, is deemed a moral failing. The body is judged as a calling card and signal as to how one is to be seen and valued."[1]

---

1. Orbach, S. (2023) 'How Rubenesque became a dirty word,' *The Telegraph*. https://www.telegraph.co.uk/art/what-to-see/how-rubenesque-became-a-dirty-word/

The context of the culture you grew up in has far-reaching implications for the way you dress and behave today. There are rules to follow, methods to learn. You're seeking yourself in the programmes, strategies, and hacks designed to keep you in a loop of dependence, spending £997 or £111 on courses you don't need to find out information you already know. You're primed to search for answers in someone else's style guidelines, someone else's social media strategy, someone else's recipe book, someone else's perfectly choreographed dance routines.

We seek connection but distrust it

You distrust other women – you deflect their compliments and say, "This old thing?" It's not only because you feel awkward in your skin (as if that is a simple concept to unpack), but because you're wondering if there's an ulterior motive to their words.

You've got scars from the memory of being eight years old and Laura Whatsherface hiding your clothes in the girls' changing room, or laughing at you during dance class; girls whispering about you and calling you names. You still hurt from the way your caregivers watched what you ate like a hawk, giving you a different meal than your siblings, smacking your hand away from the biscuits, or looking disapprovingly at what you wore.

Today you put yourself in spaces with other women because you're seeking closeness and connection; but deep inside you distrust it. Your relationships with other women have been marred by wounding, thanks to the betrayal you feel in the one relationship with a woman that was supposed to be about unconditional love. And it isn't simply the way women in your close environment were treated or how they treated you.

As you're working through this book, keep in mind the context of the time in which you live.

This morning as I opened my laptop to work on these pages, I wound up on Instagram (how does that happen?) and came across a snippet from a TV show I had forgotten (consciously, at least) watching as a child.

In 2001, the pop band Hear'Say was formed on *Popstars* and one of the contestants, Kym Marsh, 24 years old at the time, was called "fat" by judge Nigel Lythgoe.[2] The scenes aired in a follow-up documentary, *The Hear'Say Story*, with Nigel telling Kym: "It's alright saying, 'Christmas was there.' But the goose has gotten fat."

Looking shocked, Kym asks: "Do you think I'm fat?"

Nigel tells the young mum: "I think you've put weight on over Christmas and I [thought] you needed to lose weight before."

Conversations like this may be long forgotten, but they play on repeat like a backing song in your subconscious. Aged 10, you watched this on TV and the belief was formed: a woman who looks like that is fat and fat is bad and I must not let myself go.

Then you wonder why, every Christmas, you have the same boring conversation with yourself about what you will and won't eat. Why you go on diet after diet, never satisfied with the result. You wonder why you hate yourself when you eat pizza, or can't stop focusing on your thighs on the sun lounger for long enough to enjoy your holiday.

---

2. Myleene Klass, Instagram, August 2025. Original footage *The Hear'Say Story*, ITV 2001.

Where did it all go wrong?

That *I'm Too Sexy* dance was the last time I remember feeling unapologetically joyful in my body – until the comments about my belly began. The little belly that once felt a part of me became a battleground and symbol of everything I was taught to hate about myself. It's no surprise that by the time I stood in a dance class, I'd already learned to distrust my body's natural rhythms.

Dance, which should have been joyful, became another area of judgement.

Individual dancers have been credited with creating dancing concepts, but the act itself is a human form of self-expression. Nobody owns it. Your body can move however the fuck you want your body to move. In joy. In celebration. With emotion. With feeling. It is compelled to jerk and kick and jump however it feels. Dance began as something wild, free, and deeply human.

So where did it all go wrong?

At some point, somebody came up with the concept of ballet. Someone invented tap. Somebody took this natural form of self-expression and turned it into an industry.[3] And then other people took those concepts, and sold us the dream, with music boxes that played *Swan Lake*, featuring tiny ballerinas twirling endlessly; an ornament found in every little girl's bedroom in the 1980s and '90s.

They did the same to dance as they did to style: a wonderful form of self-expression, a beautiful tool for actualisation, a powerful business strategy – turned into the oppressor. Turned into a source of frustration and shame. And just like dance is

---

3. You can read more about the origin and history of ballet in *Apollo's Angels: A History of Ballet* by Jennifer Homans.

inherent in your humanness, so is using your clothes as communication. But somewhere along the line, in your lifetime or someone else's, the message was relayed that you're doing it wrong, and the goalposts are always moving. Just as I practised twirling and twirling, always to be told I was getting it wrong, you're buying and buying clothes, always to feel like you never nail it.

Over the years, I have thought often about the woman who, every January, would poke me in my little belly and call me a "fat thing" as I stood in front of her in my little knickers in her freezing maisonette in Portsmouth city centre. I used to be angry. I could see how her behaviour towards me set into motion a series of events in my life which I felt I deserved because I wasn't good enough.

But now, when I see the memory, I am not the little girl. I am an observer watching this exchange with sadness – but knowing that aside from inventing a time machine and the ability to clone myself, run into that room, grab little me and take her the fuck away from there, I have done all I can to rescue her.

Maybe now I see the memory from a different perspective because, in some ways, I have changed it.

When I think of that woman, I wonder, without emotion, what must have happened to her when she was four or five years old to make her believe this. What experiences caused her to be so emotionally stunted that she thought it was fine to say such things to a child? I could hold onto anger at that 60-year-old woman. But it wouldn't really be a 60-year-old woman I was angry at; it would be the five-year-old she once was who got this lesson from somewhere. It isn't our responsibility to make sense of what happened to the people who hurt us, or to fix it for them, or even to forgive them. We don't have to forgive damaging behaviour, and we don't have to forget. But we can make the decision that their trauma does not become our trauma.

If that woman was 60 when I was four, that would mean she was born in 1929. If the person who was 60 when *she* was four taught her that *her* body was wrong, they were born in 1869. I am unwilling to let something from the 1800s impact my experience here *today*. The best thing I can do for the woman who made me feel this way about myself, and the woman who made her feel that way, is release it.

There is no point being angry at the individual, because that changes nothing. As the saying goes, holding a grudge is like drinking poison and hoping the other person dies.

We win by one) living on purpose in ways that completely defies expectations of who we could be and two) – most importantly – challenging the deep-rooted, systemic issues that caused this in the first place.

By doing this work – this painful, confronting, often laborious and always relentless work – we ensure that little girls born today never lose their *I'm Too Sexy* feeling. Exploring your relationship with style and self is the first step. How far do you think you can get by following someone else's rules? How much money can you make when your self-expression is capped to the level at which your coach (who's replaced your dance teacher) says is acceptable?

You're asking "Does this look OK?" or "Have I done this right?" about things you fucking love wearing – because you used to spend your Saturdays staring at a wall.

Just Get Dressed: End of chapter task

Psychologists have found that our core beliefs are formed by age seven.[4] These inform our habits and behaviours, they shape the way we view the world, and what we believe ourselves capable of.

We delete, distort, and generalise the world around us based on our core beliefs.

If your core belief is "my body is wrong" then you are less likely to want to draw attention to yourself, believe yourself capable of extraordinary things, or advocate for yourself. At best, it stops you achieving your potential. At worst, it can make you vulnerable to abuse. It's like you're running but on a treadmill, always striving to get somewhere but always ending up in the same place. And it always leaves you looking outside yourself for the answer.

This task is designed to draw out the moments of your life when your beliefs about your style, self-expression, and your body were formed. The core memory may be hiding under other experiences.

For example, you may remember something that happened aged twenty-four, but that's not the core experience. That's an experience layered on top of the core, which confirms the belief the core experience gave you.

This is a chunky task, so we'll break it down into steps. Ideally, you'll complete these in one session, but if you need to take breaks and come back to it, that's fine. The important thing is

---

4. Heiphetz, L. *et al.* (2012) 'The development of reasoning about beliefs: Fact, preference, and ideology,' *Journal of Experimental Social Psychology*, 49(3), pp. 559–565. https://doi.org/10.1016/j.jesp.2012.09.005.

doing the task and not putting this on a shelf somewhere, forgetting all about it, and continuing with the same wardrobe habits that brought you to this book in the first place.

Step one: Identify the belief

What is the overarching feeling or belief I have about myself [style/body/general] that I would like to let go of?

You might write a sentence or a few words. Maybe it manifests as a feeling in your body, or looks like a colour or shape. Your mind is an incredible tool with its own ways of thinking and framing. Don't make the way it processes the belief "wrong."

Step two: Remember a time without it

You may have lived out this core belief for many years, but there was a time before it. No baby is born thinking how ugly or how stupid they are. Those come later with exposure to certain environments, incidents, or repeated messages.

Ask yourself:

- Can I remember a time I lived *without or before* this feeling?
- What was that like?
- How did I feel instead?

Step three: Find the origin

Ask yourself:

- Can I remember with specificity the first time I felt this way?

- Can I recall the moment this belief was formed, and that I first felt this feeling?
- What happened? Where was I, what was happening, how old was I, and what was I wearing?
- If I close my eyes and scan my body, where in my body does this feeling live?

Step four: create two timelines

Now work backwards from today to the moment of the core memory. On a piece of paper, draw a timeline (however makes sense to you) and on that timeline, starting with the present moment, mark significant events that have affirmed the core belief created in that original moment.

Once you have this timeline, draw a new one. On this new timeline, you're going to do the same thing, except this time, you're looking for moments that affirmed the *opposite belief* of the core memory.

For example, let's say your core memory is being laughed at on non-school-uniform day aged six, so from then on you've believed you don't have any style. Your original timeline pinpoints all the moments you've been trained to look out for as confirmation of that original belief. But there will have been plenty of other moments that demonstrate you *do* have style – the compliment from the stranger on the train about your boots. Your friend asking to borrow a dress because "you always have the best things." The meeting you walked into feeling killer, because of the outfit you wore.

Creating this second timeline will likely take significantly longer than the first, because it requires you to go back into your experiences and look for what was there that you didn't see before. It's worth the time, though. Because whether it's an hour or a week, you will be surprised by how much information you have available to you that cancels out your core belief.

Step five: Reframe the belief

Once you have this information, ask yourself this question:

Given the discovery of this new information, what new, positive, and more helpful belief can I choose to have about my style instead?

Use this new belief as an affirmation. Save it on your phone. Repeat it in the mirror. You'll be surprised how soon this becomes your new thought-pattern with committed, repetitive practice.

Honour your younger self

This is an additional task you might choose to do in order to help you affirm your new positive beliefs.

Find a photo of yourself around the age of a significant experience that gave you the core beliefs you carry today about what you can wear or who you can be.

Get it printed and put it in a nice frame. Place it somewhere where you see it regularly. I have mine on my desk – she's in my peripheral vision as I write this book. No it's not weird; yes, you do have time.

Take it out of the time you would have spent staring at a wall of clothes thinking, "What the hell should I wear today?"

Prompts:

- Imagine she's standing in front of you – what do you want her to know?
- If you'd been an adult when she was a child, what words of encouragement and support would you give her?
- What does she need to know about the experiences for which she made herself the problem?
- What lessons does she have for you?

Now every time you have a negative thought about yourself, imagine saying it to her.

Imagine saying it to a little girl. If you wouldn't say it to her, don't say it to yourself. You think of yourself as a grown-ass woman, but somewhere inside, likely within your relationship to style and self, that little girl still exists.

What can you do to honour her today?

Just for a minute today if that's all you have, make decisions as if you were her. I'm not suggesting you have a massive tantrum in the middle of the supermarket like an actual five-year-old. But rather ask yourself; what did she do for the sheer joy of it? What can you do today, tomorrow, and every day for the rest of your life to live with childlike wonder?

It could be as simple as picking up some flowers for yourself when you do go to the supermarket. Or turning off your phone for five minutes as you enjoy your coffee. Playing a song you love and dancing like your life depends on it, limbs flailing everywhere, without fear you're getting it wrong. Maybe it's drawing, or cutting and sticking to create an unhinged and inexplicable collage.

Chapter 5

The Dick-Covered Lab Coat

Wearing your working-class roots can feel like wearing a cone of shame.

My mum had been called into my school because I had been accused of plagiarism. Apparently my English essay was *that* good – written in class at a time *before* the internet was easily accessible on mobile phones – that it aroused suspicion.

The subtext of the conversation was: *a kid from a place like this can't be that intelligent.*

Despite my determination, at 11 years old, I had just about experienced enough to make me feel like giving up. Our primary schools had been OK – our secondary school made "requires improvement" look like an understatement.

Lots of the friends I'd had since nursery were skipping class, smoking, getting into fights, and who knows what else. So my mum lied about our address and got me into the "good" school some miles away. I remember her telling me off for missing a "t" from the name of the town she said our house was in on my student planner.

The standard of teaching might have been better at my new school, but the bullying was worse.

I was put into classes with children whose life experience was very different from mine and they would not let Fat Sam the

Grover forget it. Because money wasn't much of an issue for the families whose children went to this school, the uniform required was substantial. Every item had to have the logo, which meant you couldn't buy the cheaper jumpers from Tesco, they had to come from a specific supplier at about five times the price, unless you wanted to risk detention. This was very stressful for my parents, because at this point we didn't have much money.

I remember the Christmas before, my dad was working as a milkman and people gave him tips. My sisters and I sat on the living room floor opening envelopes, mostly containing coins and the occasional £5 note, and we thought we were rich.

A few weeks into my time at this new school, someone stole my uniform from the changing room when I was in PE class. Then another pupil drew giant dicks all over my lab coat. They ruined the thing I was required to bring to science lessons. If I didn't wear my lab coat, I'd face detention.

My mum tried her best to get rid of the dicks but of course it felt like my fault. Not that she said it, but I felt like if only I hadn't been so dorky or unpopular or fat – I had been put on a diet the year before – then maybe this wouldn't have happened. Despite several hot washes, you could always see the faint outlines of the dicks. Because money was tight and there were three of us, my sisters had my hand-me-downs.

Five years later, my youngest sister was wearing a lab coat covered in the faint outlines of dicks.

Transformation is an internal job

This is not a book about social mobility, it's about clothes – but clothes, as we've discovered, do tell the story of social mobility. Wearing your working class roots is like wearing that lab coat, except you never get to shrug it off. And that's important, because it shapes your self-concept.

In the 1950s, a plastic surgeon named Maxwell Maltz noticed the lives of some patients would change dramatically post-surgery, whilst others would remain the same.[1] He observed how some patients would look in the mirror after undergoing surgery like rhinoplasty and see no change, despite the sometimes dramatic physical difference. Maltz realised these patients couldn't outrun their self-concept. They may have been looking into an external mirror, but they also had an internal one which reflected back to them their beliefs. He concluded that transformation was an internal job. For a person to truly change, they must change their inner self-image.

If your internal mirror reflects poverty, or ugliness, or shame then your brain will find ways to keep rerunning the same story.

Maltz said change doesn't happen through repetition of words; it's a synthetic experience. He developed a technique called "theatre of the mind," stating that your mind can't tell the difference between a lived experience and a mental one. He realised that all day every day, humans run stories in their heads like movies. If you can enter the theatre of the mind, you can direct a new and intentional story. He suggested that for a minimum of 21 days (yep, that's where "it takes 21 days to form a habit" comes from) we carry out a mental rehearsal of how we want to feel. We can project any new vision from the mind theatre onto our physical lives.

Without pretending there aren't systemic issues at play, or that privilege isn't a thing, this is a tool you can use to improve your

---

1. Maltz, M. (2015) *Psycho-Cybernetics: Updated and Expanded*. Penguin.

self-concept and mentally move yourself out of where you're still living.

So whilst we do the internal work, let's take a look at some of those systemic issues.

Class, power, and style

In July 2024, the UK got a new government following a general election. Prime Minister Keir Starmer appointed Angela Rayner as deputy. Rayner became a mum at 16, brought up on a council estate, was told she'd never amount to anything – but became deputy prime minister.[2] She is a Labour politician, but the essence of this story is surely true conservatism, because it's someone pulling themselves out of social welfare and becoming independently wealthy.

On her first day on the job, Rayner wore a £550 suit from British brand Me + Em. No, it shouldn't have been a story… *but it was.* And it was a story because what you wear carries extra baggage when you add in class and gender. I want to live in a society where people are judged solely on merit and not on their trousers, but we can't get there by refusing to acknowledge the true translation of the hard-hitting headlines about Rayner's suit.

ME+EM, the brand which manufactured the suit, is fairly transparent (in the grand scheme of fashion) on its ethics and sustainability. It's part of the Ethical Trading Initiative, requires all suppliers to be members of SEDEX, donates its offcuts and gives proceeds to Smart Works. It's a UK brand that, at the time of being worn by Rayner, had just gone international.

Studies show that those perceived to be up-to-date with style are

---

2. https://www.angelarayner.co.uk/about/

seen as having up-to-date skills. Better than a deputy prime minister stuck in the past, no? Better than a deputy prime minister wearing a non-UK brand on her first day in the job, no? Better than a deputy prime minister walking round in Chinese-owned, ethically-dubious Shein, for her first day as second-in-command of the UK, no?

When you're a working class woman, the answer is a definitive NO.

Several commentators made the point that Keir Starmer's wife, Victoria, had also worn Me + Em for the couple's first official appearance at Downing Street, but the discourse regarding her style had been much more favourable. Her outfit was called "aspirational and approachable" in *The Times*.

Why the difference in tone?

It comes down to power.

At the time of the controversy, the UK had a gender-balanced Cabinet for the first time – up from 24 per cent women in 2019, to nearly 50 per cent after the last election. This contributed to the UK's leap from 14th to fourth in the overall gender parity rankings for 2025, the biggest jump among advanced economies.

Whilst the role of the prime minister's partner is often one of diplomacy, the role of the deputy prime minister is making decisions. Should anything happen to the prime minister, the deputy takes the helm. If we read between the lines – if we look at what's not being said as much as what is – what we see is fear from the establishment.

Firstly, Victoria Starmer has been clear that she doesn't want publicity and she doesn't want power. She's playing the "dutiful wife" role.

Angela Rayner, on the other hand, is in a position of power. This desire for power goes against everything women have been told they should be for centuries: unthinking, passive, spoken *to*, not speaking. There is a particular snobbery and ridicule reserved for working class women who achieve social mobility and dare to have ambitions outside the limitations assumed of their upbringing.

The problem isn't Angela Rayner as a *person*, or even her outfit; it's what she represents.

When Hannah Spencer, a plumber by trade, won the by-election for Gorton and Denton as a Green Party candidate in February 2026, commentary on her outfits ranged from "children's TV presenter" to "traitor to her working-class roots."

I know what it is to feel like you don't fit in; like the success you have achieved and now wear as an outfit is a betrayal of where you come from. In spaces of historic wealth and privilege, though, your "working-class roots" outfit may as well be a sandwich board saying "I don't belong here."

It was rarely a problem when Boris Johnson scruffed up his appearance to appear like a man of the people, leaning on working-class stereotypes to sell them ideas that ultimately left us all worse off. Writing in *The Guardian*, Charlie Porter noted:

> "The suits that Johnson wears are no joke. They maintain a language of patriarchal power that has its roots in colonialism and empire [...] Men's clothes – aren't they so funny? Novelty socks, comedy ties, hopeless style. How we laugh, without interrogating the language clothes play in maintaining patriarchy. Yet the joke continues to be on us."

Women from working–class backgrounds who've risen to positions of power likely have a lot of ideas about the way things could change to benefit more people, hence what drove them against the odds to get there. Research tells us women are more likely to give to charity than men, and to more causes. They are also more likely to want to be involved in charitable endeavours and involve their families in a way men are less likely to do.

They also don't want to do jobs the way they've seen them done before.

Breaking the cycle

When I became the first female editor of a group of newspapers, I faced a backlash. My only example of editors up to that point had been men. I witnessed behaviour in newsrooms that was often scary, threatening, or created a tense atmosphere. There were certain male characters you could not approach with bad news, because they'd go off on one. These men were always placated by women, who became the protectors of their peace. They would whisper: 'He's so stressed, I wouldn't go in there if I were you, he's got so much on,' when you approached the door.

I did not want to do that job as I'd seen it done. I wanted to create a collaborative, kinder environment that was more representative of the country. The media is notoriously elitist, and despite apprenticeship schemes and various initiatives, the majority of the top national journalists and columnists are privately educated.

I knew it would be different for me because, like Ms Rayner, and Ms Spencer, I was often reminded of my unsuitability for the task, given my vagina and my background.

Just Get Dressed

At a work Christmas party, shortly after my promotion was announced, one of those same women who excused emotional behaviour from men (because emotion is only labelled emotion when it's a woman crying, not a man screaming) said to me: 'Everyone thinks you're a bitch [for getting that job].'

I had no more than exchanged a polite "hello" with this woman up to that point. And I had not yet worked a single day in my new role. Yet, without my knowledge, I'd already been judged to a standard I had no idea existed. I tried to think about how my behaviour could have been perceived as bitch-like. And what is a bitch?

During my time at this newspaper, I'd spearheaded a campaign to help persecuted immigrants, raised money for children in care, investigated alleged corruption at the council and even went on assignment as a firefighter. I trained to go into burning buildings to save lives, and here I was – a fucking bitch.

The only things I could conclude had warranted such a title was that I'd displayed ambition and I wore stylish clothes.

One moment that defined my current career was having a coat tossed at me. The director I was meeting shook hands with my male deputy and didn't even look at me, save for swinging his jacket in my direction. I realise now that I wasn't dressed for the role. I don't know if the jacket tossing would have happened whatever I wore, but that was the last time I dressed humbly in any job.

When I was receiving abuse online (like the time a thread about my boobs on an article that had nothing to do with my boobs garnered over 100 comments) a male colleague – unusually perceptive – said to me: 'We are at the same level, but I see how much more abuse you get than me. And the only difference between us is that you're a woman, and I'm a man.'

As I was writing this chapter, I asked my audience about the double-standards they'd faced when dressing for work.

One woman said: 'I refused to wear heels on a 12hr shift because my male counterpart didn't have to. It was considered the "norm" at the time for women to have to wear stiletto based shoes whereas the men didn't. I challenged it on the grounds it wasn't part of the uniform policy and had no bearing on role ability. They fired me.'

Another was told to tone it down because "you won't be taken seriously."

Another recounted the time a potential business partner spent the meeting staring at her boobs, then made a lewd comment in earshot of her boss. Afterwards, when she said how upset she was, she was told, 'This is an important contract for us, I hope you're not suggesting it will be a problem.'

Whenever I am told to stop giving airtime to the problematic rhetoric I see rising up across social media about a woman we think has too much power and the associated commentary on her clothes, I feel a duty to do it louder.

Part Two

The World You're Dressing In

History, power, politics, gender, industry, and current affairs are converging in your closet.

Getting dressed is rarely a case of simply selecting an outfit. It's identity selection, assimilation, and a statement, whether made consciously or not, about how you define yourself and the society in which you live.

Your wardrobe is not only a mirror of your beliefs, it's a mirror to the state of the world. And when that world is in flux, no wonder you find it hard to define your personal style.

Let's also consider how outside influence has more bearing on your style today than ever before. Prior to the internet, you could shut the door to your house and sink into privacy. Now you have a virtual window open 24/7, giving you access to outside influences that distract you, make you question yourself, and have you spending money on items you don't really need.

Just Get Dressed

You think the outfit you've chosen is separate from "out there" but the relationship between your wardrobe and society is symbiotic.

Chapter 6

Steve Jobs is Not Your Idol

The "I don't care what I wear" stance is a power move that only works for people who already have power.

"You shouldn't care about what you wear. Caring is uncool. I made £10,000 today and I'm dressed in a bin bag."

Spend more than 30 seconds on LinkedIn and you're bound to come across this rhetoric. And the poster boy held up for why what you wear doesn't matter, referenced over and over again to shut down any nuanced dialogue about style? Steve Jobs.

According to some, the fact Steve Jobs had a uniform of black mock turtleneck and jeans meant he didn't care about what he wore. There are two problems with this assumption.

1. It fails to address Jobs' substantial privileges which meant he was able to create a uniform and wear it on repeat without career damage.
2. Steve Jobs isn't an example of someone who didn't care what he wore. He's an example of someone who did.

Do a quick Google image search for Steve Jobs in the 1970s and 1980s and you'll find images of a man dressed in the workwear of the time: plaid shirts, ties, dress shoes.

The cognitive load of what to wear

Jobs was concerned about the cognitive load of choosing what to wear.

In the 1980s, he became interested in a uniform jacket made for Sony workers by Japanese designer Issey Miyake. According to his biographer, Walter Isaacson, Jobs liked what the uniform stood for (corporate bonding) and he suggested something similar for Apple employees, which did not go down well. Still, Jobs and Miyake became friends and Jobs adopted the black mock turtleneck as his signature look. Why?

According to the New York Times: "It was a garment that did away with an extraneous fold at the neck, that had the ease of a T-shirt and a sweatshirt but also the cool, minimal lines of a jacket."[1]

Miyake made Jobs "like a hundred of them," Isaacson noted. The black mock turtleneck became synonymous with Jobs. What an excellent branding tool. Even today, the image of Jobs in that style has been baked into culture so deeply that you only have to see a black mock turtleneck and you think of him. And because of the uniformity of his style, from the 1980s right up until his death in 2011, people use him as an example of why what you wear doesn't matter.

But this is a man who proved it did.

Jobs was interested in uniform because he wanted to unburden himself from the cognitive load of having to choose what to wear every day. It's an approach that has been adopted since by the

____

1. Cramer, J. (2020) 'Why Steve Jobs chose this designer's turtlenecks,' *The New York Times.* https://www.nytimes.com/2022/08/10/style/issey-miyake-steve-jobs-black-turtleneck.html

likes of Barack Obama and Mark Zuckerberg (who we'll come onto in a moment).

There is privilege in genuinely not having to care about what you wear, and being able to wear the same thing on repeat without it harming your reputation, but rather enhancing it. There is also privilege in being able to buy multiples of a top which currently retails at £490.[2]

This is not a privilege many women, or minoritised groups, have.

In the UK, the median hourly earnings for women working full-time, excluding overtime, was £17.88.[3] You'd have to work 27 hours to afford one turtleneck.

Have they run out of clothes?

In 2024, newsreaders at Canadian channel *Global News BC* conducted an on-air "sociological experiment" to highlight the double standards for men and women dressing at work. A similar experiment had been done in 2014 by Australian news anchor Karl Stefanovic.[4] He wore the same blue suit for a year.

'No-one has noticed,' he said. 'But women, they wear the wrong colour and they get pulled up. They say the wrong thing and there's thousands of tweets written about them.'

In the new version of the experiment, the Canadian news anchors wore the same outfits on repeat for a week. During the

---

2. https://uk.isseymiyake.com/collections/black-turtleneck-top?srsltid=Afm
BOoqpq3aOfUWFhKlHJvlezYZ896kxQrvNu2YkOD2TGSUioSARNxQm
3. House of Commons, 2024.
4. BBC News (2014) *Australian TV host wears same suit for a year and nobody notices*. https://www.bbc.co.uk/news/newsbeat-30069564.

first week, morning anchor Jason Pires and evening anchor Chris Gailus repeated their suits without viewer response. The following week, Sophie Lui along with Sonia Sunger, Katelin Owsianski, and Kristi Gordon each wore the same outfit during their broadcasts.

According to Sophie Lui, the channel did not receive one email about the male news anchors repeating outfits. But viewers noticed, and wrote in about, the female news anchors doing the same. Shared on Lui's Instagram comments[5] included, "Is this some sort of protest?" and "Have they run out of clothes?" In her post about the experiment, Lui said it was positive that most of the comments were curious rather than negative. But the point remains – people *noticed*.

Women are held to not just a higher standard than men, but a standard that keeps moving. Unspoken expectation (unspoken so long as you are sticking to the rules) means we are not only supposed to be good at our jobs, and do far more pastoral care at work, we also have to think more about our clothes. This eats into the time we can spend prepping for meetings, studying for new qualifications and generally advancing in our careers.

Who is teaching us these things?

And then there is the privilege of being white and wealthy, which means some women face less scrutiny than others.

As part of my work, I speak at events and help companies and recruiters with workwear policy. I often hear stories of candidates being rejected based on what they wear. One example

---

5. https://www.instagram.com/sophielui/

that has stuck with me is a young Black man turned down by a legal firm because he was wearing "the wrong colour shoes."

When you don't grow up in an environment where your adults are in the corporate world and there is no conversation about workwear, and instead the conversation is shrouded in the stress of never having enough money, of course it skews the odds against you when you later interview for corporate roles.

Recently I pondered this on LinkedIn and one well-meaning gentleman told me it was the responsibility of the individual and they should have "learned about this in school." My response was… they should learn about this in school. But they don't. Not unless they're at a private school or non-government curriculum school where there are additional resources or classes.

Some 57 per cent of peers in the House of Lords were privately educated, compared to seven per cent of the population.[6] They have a skillset that feels inherent as it's simply part of the environment they've been in.

It's akin to picking up a language. If you moved somewhere with a dialect different than yours, or a language you didn't speak and you didn't have a copy of *[Language] for Dummies* or hadn't downloaded Duolingo, you'd slowly begin to understand words and phrases until eventually, you'd be able to have a full-blown conversation. But at first you'd have no clue what was being said and it would take a lot longer than if you had the guidebook or an app to translate for you.

Acknowledging how your background, gender, abilities, and experiences impact how you dress (and how you feel about

---

6. *Labour blasts 'closed elite' as figures reveal majority of House of Lords went to private school* (2020). https://www.politicshome.com/news/article/labour-blasts-closed-elite-as-figures-reveal-majority-of-house-of-lords-went-to-private-school.

getting dressed) is vital if you want to improve your relationship with clothes.

When the majority of hiring and firing decision-makers are still those who've benefitted from an intersection of privileges which means no one has ever turned them down because of their shoes – whether because of how they are perceived *or* that they've been in environments which mean what to wear for corporate life is second nature – we need to talk about it.

We have a long way to go

Sixty per cent of men think women already have equal job opportunities. This only takes into account gender, not race.[7] A 2017 study showed people's biases. One hundred students were given the same descriptions of professors, with two crucial details changed – the professors' race and clothing. When asked which professor they thought would be most trustworthy, they were less likely to trust the Black professor and would show them less respect.

According to Professor Keon West, author of *The Science of Racism*, researchers found that whilst students were more likely to trust the white professor when he was dressed casually, the opposite was true for the Black professor.[8]

High-end fashion's acknowledgement of Black people happened only as recently as the 1990s. In a documentary about *Vogue*, Anna Wintour explains how up until the emergence of hip-hop,

7. Brenan, M. (2021) 'Gender disparities in views of women's equality persist,' *Gallup.com*, 15 October. https://news.gallup.com/poll/355958/gender-dispari ties-views-women-equality-persist.aspx.
8. Aruguete, M.S., Slater, J. and Mwaikinda, S.R. (2017) 'The Effects of Professors' Race and Clothing Style on Student Evaluations,' *The Journal of Negro Education*, 86(4), p. 494. https://doi.org/10.7709/jnegroeducation.86.4.0494.

fashion was selling an "American dream… but it was a white one."

In the documentary, stylist Misa Hylton and singer Mary J Blige recalled how they went to a boutique and at the register, the card they were using kept declining. Hylton called the bank and was told there was no issue with the card, it wasn't actually being rung up by the sales assistant. "It was because we were young and we were Black… you see how luxury fashion brands didn't value us or respect us and they didn't really see their brands on us," said Hylton.

Hypocrisy is evident in the way the highest echelons of fashion borrow styles of dress from "the street", sell them to consumers who can afford elevated pricing, and act like this is revolutionary fashion. Jeroen van den Broek, criminologist and researcher at Erasmus School of Law, says certain groups "experience exclusion, while perversely enough style elements from their street culture are used in commerce to present them with social goals that everyone should meet."[9]

In other words, the wrong people make money from street culture. Massive companies take ideas that originate on the street and make money from them without credit. White men specifically have been able to borrow codes of dress from those perceived to have less status or socio-economic power.

Data-mining wannabe-president Mark Zuckerberg used clothes to appear as your friendly neighbourhood IT nerd, rather than a power-hungry money-maker. But notice how Zuck still obeys the codes of dress when he's being hauled in front of governments or at black tie events.

---

9. *De sociëteit | NPO Start* (no date). https://npo.nl/start/afspelen/de-soci
eteit_30.

No-one who is rich does not think about, or care about, their appearance.

When someone is on LinkedIn in their PJs shaming you for wanting to invest in your style because "yolo, I don't give a fuck and I still make money," think a bit deeper about why they're saying this. Likely, they've got some sort of £997 content programme to flog you, promising the one top secret formula you don't know for virality.

They're also benefitting from an intersection of privileges which mean they *can* wear an old hoodie and still make money – whether it's able-bodied, white, heteronormative, socio-economic (because there's never any mention of living rent-free thanks to daddy's money) or attractiveness – they're never acknowledging their leg up.

Turning up five minutes late with unbrushed hair for an interview you've not prepped for might be fine for Lord X the Third whose godparent owns the company, but it won't be the same for us. So what do we do? Decide to opt out, don a potato sack, and start our own society in the woods?

Chances are, you kind of *like* your life. You don't want to sack society off completely. There are some aspects that are desperately in need of improvement, for sure – but by now you recognise your own complexity and contradictions and want to be able to enjoy your style whilst also being a person of substance.

I think the answer is continuing to have the conversation. Gently correct the idea that Steve Jobs didn't care about what he wore when you hear it.

Chapter 7

You're Dressing
to Outdated Rules

Where do dress codes come from? Who wrote them? And why is it so hard, yet important, to trace their origins?

Until the mid-1970s, police women had to wear skirts, not trousers. Even when trousers were introduced for patrol work, the rule was only for night shift or winter.[1] Sexism in workplace uniforms was banned in 2018, but the Trades Union Congress (TUC) and Unison say it can still be a problem.[2]

Of course it feels challenging to be a woman dressing for work when the concept of women in boardrooms and as business owners is relatively new.

The COVID-19 pandemic shifted many things about work culture, including the way we dress. But employees, managers, and recruiters often share their frustrations with me that whilst informally things are more relaxed, employers are super slow in making formal changes. In the last four talks I've done, I've asked all the women in the room how many have received support with their style at work. Of a total 430 women, four said they had received employer paid-for help.

---

1. *History of women in policing* (no date). https://gmpmuseum.co.uk/collection-item/history-of-women-in-policing/#:~:text=Skirts%20were%20the%20norm%20for.
2. Betteley, C. (2021) *Sexism: Can my employer make me wear make-up and heels?* https://www.bbc.co.uk/news/uk-wales-58086061.

'We've got people coming in like they're ready for Royal Ascot and others like they've just rolled out of bed,' one manager told me recently. When I asked why they didn't feel able to address it, they said: 'I have no clue what I'm supposed to be wearing to work, I don't feel supported having those conversations when there's no direction from above.'

This gives way to bigger, more philosophical questions about how we "should" dress for work and life. Where do the rules come from? And does everything have a shelf-life?

Even things we consider staple now, might just be in the middle of a very very long trend cycle. The suit as we know it today originated in the 18th Century when opulence began to fade out in favour of Enlightenment values – sobriety, practicality, and modesty. It was a staple of workwear from the late 1890s-2019, but when even British high street stalwart Marks & Spencer stopped selling suits in-store, we have to think about the idea of permanence and transience in style. Maybe it's not that the suit is here to stay, but that we're simply living in the time period of it as a long-term trend.

And as for "dress codes"? Don't get me started.

Dress for success

Post-Second World War, as women began entering the male-dominated corporate workspace, it became necessary to adopt some elements of how men dressed. In the late 1970s, dress codes for women in corporate settings were formalised in *The Woman's Dress For Success Book* (ick) by John T Molloy. Whilst his work has been criticised, some people suggest it's not Molloy who's the problem, he's simply the bearer of information.

I am no longer surprised when I work with teams who have no idea where the rules they're dressing to come from. I don't raise an eyebrow when I ask: 'Who wrote this dress code document?' and people shrug. If the person writing your company workwear rules is simply regurgitating information, assuming what the rules are, and asking you to follow along without context, it creates a culture of confusion.

And competition.

Chapter 8

Compare and Despair

Comparison culture, misogyny, and the commodification of our bodies shape not just what we wear, but how we see ourselves and each other.

Jen versus Angelina.

Kate versus Meghan.

SJP versus Kim Cattrall.

We continuously pit powerful women against one another, the subtext being: wealth, money, and power comes at the expense of sisterhood. What if this is propaganda designed to keep us apart, because together we are extremely powerful?

Divide and conquer: the media's strategy

Let's use Meghan Markle as our case study. "Shameless," "bizarre," and "Montecito Marie Antoinette" are some of the headlines about her just from the past 24 hours. Clickbait, like she says, has huge financial implications. If someone's name is clickable, more headlines are generated about them. And if you can put two clickable names in one headline? Laughing all the way to the bank.

There is a system that profits from our division. The more we hate-watch, the more money pours into the pockets of billionaires who own the media, and massive companies that profit from our lack of self-esteem.

Like Meghan says, it's not about her. It's not about any of these women. But it is about every young girl who sees what we do to ambitious, opinionated women. From Taylor, to Serena, to the next girl on *Love is Blind* who will have a baptism of fire into the online world of outfit scrutiny, how much are we fair game? And where is the cut-off in terms of celebrity status?

Why this matters now

The media's obsession with pitting women against each other doesn't exist in a vacuum. It thrives in a political climate where women's rights globally are under attack. That has real consequences for how we dress, how we're perceived, and how much power we're allowed to wield.

In the 2024 UK election, Reform – a party which wants to eradicate the UK's binding to the European Convention on Human Rights (the legislation that currently protects things like maternity care) – got a 14 per cent share of the votes, won five constituencies, and came second in 100 other constituencies.

In the USA, at the time of writing, Donald Trump – the first president or former president to ever be indicted, found guilty of 34 counts of fraud and currently facing five new criminal cases, who has been accused by no less than 18 women of inappropriate behaviour, including sexual harassment and assault – is president.[1]

---

1. Keneally, M. (2020) 'List of Trump's accusers and their allegations of sexual misconduct,' *ABC News*, 18 September. https://abcnews.com/Politics/list-trumps-accusers-allegations-sexual-misconduct/story?id=51956410.

If one of the most powerful offices in the world is once again held by someone caught on camera saying you can "do anything [to women]. Grab 'em by the pussy" and how is accused of assaulting a number of women... What does that tell us about the future of equality?[2]

This isn't just politics, either; it's personal. When society moves to the right, women's bodies – and what we dress them in – become battlegrounds.

Did you know that 57 per cent of Gen Z and 60 per cent of Millennials think equal rights have gone far enough?[3] And yet a study mapping 30 years across 68 countries indicated that financial crises "undermine women's participation in the formal workforce, their presence in politics, their educational attainment, and their health outcomes."

Society moves towards traditional gender roles and we see a rise in misogyny in times of economic uncertainty.

In her book *Down Girl: The Logic of Misogyny*, author Kate Manne defines misogyny not as a hatred that's harboured individually by people, but as a product of societal structures – "social systems or environments where women face hostility and hatred because they're women in a man's world – a historical patriarchy," she told *Vox*.[4] This has to be a conversation that includes *everyone*, as men who feel disenfranchised blame

---

2. TDC (2016) *Trump On Tape: I Grab Women "By The Pu**y"*. https://www.you tube.com/watch?v=WhsSzIS84ks.
3. Survey for Ipsos and the Global Institute for Women's Leadership at King's College London, conducted for International Women's Day 2023. The survey collated the responses from more than 22,500 people aged 16-74 across 32 countries.
4. Illing, S. (2020) 'What we get wrong about misogyny,' *Vox*, 7 March. https:// www.vox.com/identities/2017/12/5/16705284/elizabeth-warren-loss-2020-sex ism-misogyny-kate-manne.

women's equality over other factors that have led to the current economic and social situation.

So what does this have to do with your wardrobe? Everything. Because the more society polices women, the more we police ourselves, and each other.

The Faustian bargain of visibility

Speaking within the context of the public fall-out of the Beckhams and their son Brooklyn, journalist Marina Hyde pondered:

> "In a way, everybody has commodified themselves, and they've done it in the slipstream of huge celebrities like the Beckhams [...] This Faustian bargain with living your life in public, sometimes the devil collects on the deal."[5]

This is the deal we're all offered now, whether we're celebrities or not. In the online economy, everyone's an influencer.

Whether you have an audience of a few hundred, or millions, are you asking for scrutiny when you put yourself up for public consumption? How much choice do you have, when so much buy-in comes from how visible you are online? How much control do you have over your narrative? How much do these women benefit from online scrutiny?

Could one argue that, unlike the many preceding centuries of

---

5. Hough, L. *et al.* (2026) 'Beckham feud: Marina Hyde on why Brooklyn has gone nuclear – The Latest,' *The Guardian*, 20 January. https://www.theguardian.com/news/audio/2026/jan/20/beckham-feud-marina-hyde-on-why-brooklyn-has-gone-nuclear-the-latest.

women being persecuted and lied about, at least now we can cash in on being dragged through the proverbial mud?

When we have invested with people, we may feel like we have a right to judge them. But is what they wear really our business? And how much of what we see in the media (both traditional and social) impacts what we wear? More than we'd like to admit, if we're honest. Judging women, now as ever, is still serving as a distraction from the things that are very much our business.

It's about so much more than pockets

What to wear is a complex equation for women and minorities because of valid concerns around physical safety. Girls learn that the onus is on them to temper the behaviour of those wishing them harm, rather than on the perpetrators of harm to keep their hands to themselves. You're making a calculated assessment every time you get dressed: Will I be safe if I wear this?

This isn't paranoia, and it starts young.

Recently, parents, students, and activists have been arguing against school dress codes, with one US investigation suggesting 90 per cent of school dress codes ban clothing associated with girls.[6] Campaigners say school dress codes are inherently sexist and do not work for those who do not identify as either male or female.

There are also those who argue that uniformity teaches discipline and tempers the risk of bullying between classmates because there is no obvious sign that anyone has more or less money.

---

6. Pendharkar, E. (2024) 'School dress codes aren't fair to everyone, federal study finds,' *Education Week*, 4 June. https://www.edweek.org/leadership/school-dress-codes-arent-fair-to-everyone-federal-study-finds/2022/10.

Just Get Dressed

This is not an argument against uniforms – they can reduce cognitive load, as we've seen with Steve Jobs. It's about how you're conditioned to not only be a good girl but to take the blame or feel guilt and shame when someone else sexualises your body.

This conditioning doesn't end at school; it follows us into adulthood. Right into the pockets of our jeans.

'How has my nine month-old son got pockets in his clothes and I'm forced to shove my phone in my bra?' This was a message from a friend of mine. Memes about dresses with pockets have been shared with humour by women since the dawn of social media. But *really*, is it so much to ask that we might have adequate storage about our person for the things we need?

And by things we need, I mean three types:

1. The items we need because we live in a world that does not accommodate our safety and bodily functions.
2. The items we *think* we need because society told us that to be a woman is to upkeep your appearance at all times.
3. The items we need because we are responsible for the care of everybody else and we are failing in our womanly role if someone asks for a tissue or a plaster and we don't have one.

It isn't simply a flaw in design which means little boys literally have more pockets in their clothes than their mothers. It speaks to a wider issue about how women are not adequately supported to fulfil their dreams. If you spend your life feeling ever-so-slightly uncomfortable, or inconvenienced, or having to make accommodations which take up precious brainpower, then you have less energy, drive, and focus to work on the things that *really* matter.

In the simple act of getting dressed, women have already exerted more mental energy than men. And this is before we go shopping – a world of random sizing labels and made-up fits. There is no mandatory guidance for manufacturers to follow when it comes to sizing and most clothing is made using an ad hoc system with no obvious relation to actual measurement, varying from country to country.

In America, "standardisation" of women's clothing sizes began in the late 1930s, as manufacturers realised they were losing millions of dollars a year by not having set sizes. Data from 15,000 American women was collected by Ruth O'Brien and William Shelton and used to create sizing standards. It was impressive work because they had no computer analysis and did it all by hand – but it was flawed. The study failed to get a cross-section of women, and most participants were white and smaller than average.[7] In the late 1940s, the system was re-worked by the Mail-Order Association of America and the National Bureau of Standards... but they based it on women in the armed forces, some of the fittest in America.

Clothing sizing for women was arbitrary, but as people got bigger, the measurements for each size changed and in the 1980s, standardisation was binned off by the American government.

In Europe in the 1990s, a standards committee set about designing a new system of labelling clothes. From 2006, this new standard supposedly began replacing older, ad hoc labelling systems, but the rate of adoption is slow and unknown. And

---

7. Stampler, L. (2026) 'The bizarre history of women's clothing sizes,' *TIME*, 13 April. https://time.com/3532014/women-clothing-sizes-history/.

here in the UK? Good luck, dolls! There is no standard for labelling. A 2023 petition was rejected by the government, which said it was not directly responsible for clothing size standardisation.[8]

Put simply: no one with the power to change anything cares that women waste time faffing about in a monotonous, frustrating daily game of will-it-won't-it-fit with their clothes.

Or maybe, just perhaps, it suits the status quo.

Unburdened by all the bullshit our male counterparts don't have to put up with, who knows what devilish ideas we may bring to fruition. Who knows what seats of power we might take. Who knows how we might change the world.

When it comes to pockets, on average they are 48 per cent shorter and 6.5 per cent narrower in women's jeans than men's.[9] According to the data, 100 per cent of men's pockets tested can fit a Samsung Galaxy phone and the iPhone X, against only 20 per cent and 40 per cent of women's pockets respectively. But I guess we are supposed to feel grateful for any pockets at all.

We may think the dearth of fully-functioning pockets is simply inconvenient, but it goes deep (far deeper than the pockets in most women's clothes). In the Middle Ages, both men and women had the same type of pocket – a pouch carried around the waist. By the early 17th Century, pockets were sewn into men's clothing. But for women, they were detachable garments worn under the layers in dresses. They gained an association

---

8. *Petition: Standardise clothing sizes across all major UK retail stores* (no date). https://petition.parliament.uk/archived/petitions/641870.
9. *Women's Pockets are Inferior.* (no date). https://pudding.cool/2018/08/pockets/.

with being amoral because you could stash letters and personal possessions in your pockets.[10]

During the French Revolution, women were banned from having pockets in case they carried revolutionary material. But in the 1800s, neoclassical, more figure-hugging dress designs became popular and there was nowhere for a pocket to hide. And of course fashion can't possibly change for *function*!

Pockets "spoilt the hang" of clothing, so women carried little bags called reticules which could fit a handkerchief, fan, and dance card. Possibly a bottle of scent. Ya know, all the essentials and by that I mean the things you need to attract men.[11] Besides, what does a woman really need pockets for anyway, when she has few civil rights and little access to money?

This is an argument women have been having for 100 years.

It's a safety issue

Recently I noticed my husband would leave his phone at home when he took our dog for a walk.

When I asked him about this, he said, 'It's really nice to be able to get a proper break and not have my phone with me.'

I pointed out that, as a woman, I do not feel safe walking the dog alone without my phone.

Every time a woman leaves the house, she is assessing her safety.

---

10. 11Alive (2021) *VERIFY: Does the lack of pockets in women's clothes link to witchcraft?* https://www.youtube.com/watch?v=H-ZIfekp15E.
11. *A Brief History of Bags and purses | Hampshire Cultural Trust Online Collections* (no date). https://collections.hampshireculture.org.uk/topic/brief-history-bags-and-purses.

And the onus is on the individual woman to keep herself safe, not on society to be safe.

Studies show the prevalence of victim-blaming, specifically when it comes to attacks on women. Of her book *Why Women Are Blamed For Everything*, Dr Jessica Taylor said: "[it] presents hundreds of studies that have consistently shown that we will pick at women and girls until we find something wrong with them, or something they did wrong – to 'explain' why they were raped or abused or even murdered."

When I hosted an all-women event, and decided on my outfit, I noticed something interesting about the way I chose my clothes. I opted for a red mini dress with a square neckline and straps. It went against the rules of what we're told are acceptable: traditionally, a stylist might say, 'If you're going low cut then do long on the bottom' or vice versa. I realised I felt safer and more confident in this outfit choice because I was going to be in a room of women.

It made me think about the disconnect between how many of the traditional styling rules are based on the interpretation of women as sexual objects for the male gaze and simultaneously are there to protect women from male behaviour.

The hourglass and the male gaze

The "hourglass" (where the shoulders and hips are relatively the same width and the waist is a percentage smaller) has been held up as the most desirable shape for women's bodies. Whether it's making a client's shoulders or hips look more narrow, or minimising a belly, in styling schools across the land you're taught to use material, colour, and lines to create the illusion of the hourglass.

Just eight per cent of women have a natural hourglass shape. So the other 92 per cent of us are supposed to spend our lives forcing our bodies into something they naturally do not want to do?

This obsession with shaping women's bodies to fit an ideal is about control, not aesthetics.

Based on my own experience and those of clients, I find women's-bodies-as-fruit-shapes more harmful than helpful, because they lead to self-objectification. In a study on objectification theory, researchers Barbara Fredrickson and Tomi-Ann Roberts write:

> "This perspective on self can lead to habitual body monitoring, which, in turn, can increase women's opportunities for shame and anxiety, reduce opportunities for peak motivational states, and diminish awareness of internal bodily states. Accumulations of such experiences may help account for an array of mental health risks that disproportionately affect women: unipolar depression, sexual dysfunction, and eating disorders."[12]

And for trans women, the stakes are even higher.

In 2025, the UK Supreme Court ruled that the definition of woman is based on biological sex. It ruled that the definition of sex as used in the Equality Act 2010 is binary and decided by biology – a person who was not born as a biological female

---

12. Fredrickson, B.L. and Roberts, T.-A. (1997) 'Objectification Theory: toward understanding women's lived experiences and mental health risks,' *Psychology of Women Quarterly*, 21(2), pp. 173–206. https://doi.org/10.1111/j.1471-6402.1997.tb00108.x.

cannot obtain the legal protections the Act affords to women by changing their gender with a Gender Recognition Certificate.

This has led to many trans women feeling unsafe in public spaces – as well as cis women who don't happen to fit the ideal of what a woman "should" look like.

You've been trained to ask for permission in a world that consistently blames you for the actions of others, and nowhere is this more evident than in the clothes we're told to wear.

The age of influence: compare and despair

What would it cost to wear the wardrobe in *Emily in Paris*? Annually, around $78,000.[13] In the 1990s, Sex and the City (SATC) started with a tiny wardrobe budget, with costume designer Patricia Field uncovering Carrie Bradshaw's famous tutu in a $5 bin. Both she and Sarah Jessica Parker have spoken about how designers would not lend clothes to this relatively-unknown after-dark show. But Carrie would still have been spending over $14,000 on clothes annually to achieve her eponymous looks. Fast-forward to *And Just Like That*, the SATC spin-off show, and the costume department borrowed $3 million of clothing to dress the main characters for one season alone.[14]

We use TV for entertainment and escapism, but in the age of streaming and social media the line between fiction and aspiration has blurred – and so has the line between inspiration and inadequacy.

---

13. Wise Finance, 2024.

14. Plummer, T. (2023) '*And just like that...* borrowed over $3 million in clothes for season two,' *Harper's BAZAAR*, 22 June. https://www.harpersbazaar.com/culture/film-tv/a44302840/and-just-like-that-season-2-costumes/.

We aren't taking the time to process, plan, or think about what our wardrobe needs. There's no thrill, experimentation or discovery in the way we shop. We are living in the Age of Influence, under the relentless pressure to keep up with the curated faux-existence of people we've never spoken to, but feel like we know, because we follow them online.

Therapists refer to this as the compare and despair cycle – the unhealthy yet ingrained habit of comparing the 3D picture of our lives, to a 2D curated snapshot into someone else's. Says psychology professor Wojciech Kaftański (*Psyche*, February 2025):

> "We [...] compare socially constructed values of status, prestige and popularity, which are essentially linked to possessing or accessing goods such as luxurious cars, swanky wardrobes or a Harvard-type education.

> "Better beats worse. That is why we often feel good when we compare ourselves with those who are worse off. We naturally find *pleasure* in the fact that we are more successful than others or that our favourite sports team beats their rivals."

But what if we refused to play this game?

From comparison to collective power

My short red dress became the least important thing about the event I hosted, but ultimately it was symbolic for the point of the day. Women saying, doing and being whatever they want without fear of judgement. And, when that judgement does unfortunately and inevitably happen, for all the reasons we've covered here, rallying together, not tearing each other apart.

Just Get Dressed

On the *Call Her Daddy* podcast, Victoria Beckham said of the Spice Girls:

> "We had the best time [...] Each girl is very different, we were five misfits that had all been told no, all been told we weren't good enough [...] but we worked together. Individually, we weren't that great, but together, we were something."

This is what I wish for all of us. Expressing our differences through our style, but working together as a collective to create something powerful.

It's #GirlPower through your clothes.

Part Three
Your Identity and Money

'I walked into Selfridges… and I walked right back out again. I kept thinking *who are you to be here?*' The words of my client, let's call her Anna to protect her privacy, a multi-six-figure executive who'd transcended all the class stereotypes we've covered to become a property owner in London.

As so many of the women who end up becoming my clients do, Anna had unfollowed me more than once on social media. She told me later it was because the questions I was asking around identity, money, womanhood, and power hit a nerve.

She had been sold on the ideology that "female" is synonymous with "martyr" and that it was shameful, silly, and frivolous to spend money on her clothes. She told herself she'd worked too hard to look like she cared about her appearance.

As we move through this section, I want you to remember this: refreshing your image will not detract from your hard work, it will illuminate it.

Chapter 9

Who's Holding
the Purse Strings?

*Your relationship with money is written all over your wardrobe and
until you examine it, it will keep sabotaging both.*

As the sales assistant wraps up your gorgeous new investment
piece, panic sets in. Suddenly your bank card feels as heavy as a
rock in your hand, you can barely lift your arm to pass it over.

This bag has been on your vision board since you were a
teenager ripping images from magazines, dreaming of the life of
a big city gal. You *finally* did it – you finally got the promotion
after working as hard as anyone you've ever known, saved the
cash, and got yourself into the store. And now your heart feels
like it might explode, but not with pride as you might have
expected; with fear and worry.

Turns out, the bag comes with a whole load of extra baggage.

What if this is all a fluke and it might go away? What if you did
something terrible at work, of which you are currently unaware,
and get fired tomorrow?

The voice of your grandad, a war gen kid who survived on
rations, comes into your head saying something about "more
money than sense." *Daily Mail* headlines hating on Meghan and
her avocados and Millennials spending their money on fancy
coffees flash before your eyes. You picture your mum's stony-
shocked face as you walk into Sunday lunch with that bag. You

101

hear your sister, covered in baby sick as *Peppa Pig* plays in the background, saying, 'It's alright for some' as if she didn't make her choices and you didn't make yours.

You start to ask yourself: But where would I wear it? What if I get mugged? What if I damage it? What if there's an apocalypse tomorrow?

And then you start to second sell yourself on this thing you've wanted for over 20 years; *it's an investment so if I keep it in the dustbag at the back of the wardrobe then one day my great granddaughter could have it* (even though you don't want children, but you only feel like you're allowed to have something, so long as there is value to a stranger you'll never meet and who may never exist).

You've used this bag as a goal to work towards. It's an emblem of what you will have achieved when you make it into Chanel. But you panic when it finally happens because you believe in some way that you'll have to exchange it for your values. Deep down, you fear that having this bag is a betrayal of your working class roots.

You picture the faces of your so-called friends, who you've noticed already aren't responding to your messages in the way they used to when you were broke. You imagine the disapproving looks of clients, who you think will be mad at you for visually glowing up. You worry they might start reddit threads about how self-absorbed you've become.

Whether you grew up in a wealthy household, but you never felt loved, so you learned that having money equals abandonment, or whether your childhood was spent in a perpetual state of struggle, so your core belief became "money is hard to make," these stories are manifesting in some way today. And always inside your wardrobe.

There is no such thing as a personal styling issue; there is only identity, mindset, and beliefs.

Here are the most common ways I see money manifest as wardrobe woe.

Issue 1: Houston, we have an inventory problem

You've neglected your style because you grew up in a household where materialism was akin to devil-worship. Perhaps the women in your life were the epitome of martyrdom, so you now believe (deep down under the layers of sub-par clothes and a bra that's seen better days) that spending money on yourself is selfish.

Or perhaps "style" was a swear word, so you never learned any of the basics, leaving you with a feeling of inadequacy that manifests as defence. You're always on the attack; *it shouldn't matter what you wear! People who care about these things have more money than sense!*

And even though you're here reading this book (which is more than can be said for most people with this underlying money belief, so kudos to you), you secretly judge yourself for it. Never mind the pang of – what is it, envy, jealousy, anger? – you feel towards other women who you perceive as showing off online with their trinkets.

Issue 2: Saving it for best

This is scarcity manifesting as a style decision. You aren't wearing the lovely things you own, instead opting for things that will do because you're scared you'll ruin the lovely things and won't be able to afford to replace them.

You have amazing pieces tucked away in the back of your wardrobe, in dustbags and boxes, never to see the light of day, which is not what the designer created them for. The problem with delaying wearing these items for a more joyful occasion is, well, that it's joyless. Your behaviour is influenced not by what you own, but by what you wear. If you're opting for sub-par over sensational, your behaviour leaves a lot to be desired. Not making the money to buy another [insert special item here] is a self-fulfilling prophecy, borne from your lack of wearing [the special item].

Issue 3: Shop 'til you drop

You've learned to use shopping as an emotional plaster. Perhaps you felt abandoned by your parents, or that they were emotionally unavailable. Maybe you grew up in a household where having new things was rare, so now that you have money, your inner child has taken full control of the purse strings, and she's buying herself anything and everything.

Shopping itself is not an issue (as we will cover later), but when it's leading to more stress, self-criticism, or shame – or worse, is putting you into financial difficulties – it does need addressing.

Issue 4: They want me to stay here

'How's your little business going?' asks uncle Barry, four stiff drinks into a family Christmas dinner as dry as the turkey (until the inevitable argument about religion or politics or aunt Susan's new boyfriend kicks off later). You nod and say, 'Yeah good thanks,' before enduring a two-hour mansplain from a man who knows as much about business as the Bethlehem donkey.

You've already toned down your outfit, left your favourite jewellery at home, and foregone your usual Moët (and the associated eyebrows raised) for something non-label. You came to the conclusion years ago that it's easier to pretend you don't have ambition than to defend it.

Maybe you don't have a family dynamic where Christmas together is even *a thing*. Maybe there are people you're blood with, who wouldn't recognise you in the street. Maybe you never go back to the streets they live on. Maybe you decided at a very young age that this was not your future, and you left, and they can't understand it. Maybe they call you a snob. They think you're a bitch.

Maybe it's your friends. You've noticed some snide remarks about the way you're dressing, the money you're making, or what you post online.

You resist spending money on your wardrobe because you worry it makes you a bad person, and will ultimately lead to your rejection. After all, the prehistoric parts of your brain equate a snide remark about your shoes to the danger of being cast out from the pack and inevitably starving, or being eaten, in the wild.

You've conditioned yourself to settle here, at just about good enough, in case taking things to another fucking stratosphere pisses people off (spoiler: it will. Good.)

But if you're being really honest, like not-worrying-about-hurting-feelings, good-girl-unleashed honest, you would never swap wardrobes with these people. If you literally wouldn't walk a mile in their shoes, don't take advice, or pay too much attention. Most judgements aren't about you, anyway.

And the truth is not nearly as nasty as you imagine. Other women are waiting for your wardrobe glow-up. They're looking for someone to go first, so they feel they have permission – in a world that's rewarded their compliance and punished their self-expression – to do the same.

So, what IS your money mindset?

Let's find out what's really going on with you and money. Answer these questions, use them as prompts to dig into your current mindset, then do the end-of-chapter task.

- Growing up, what did I learn about money? What was the feeling about money in the household I grew up in?
- What is my first memory of money? If I can't pinpoint a specific experience, can I describe a feeling about money?
- When I close my eyes and feel any restriction about money in my body, where is it? What does it feel like? Is it dull and heavy, or sharp and strong? Does it have a colour or shape?
- When I think about my relationship with money, is there anyone in particular who comes to mind?
- Complete this sentence: Money is…
- What can I choose to believe about money instead?

Just Get Dressed: End of chapter tasks

Task 1: frequency check

In the middle of a blank piece of paper, write "Current Reality" and list all the things that are currently true for you. Put down your level of income, debt, where you live, mortgage, the car you drive, the things you spend your money on, habits, relationships, job, etc.

Once you have an exhaustive list, draw a big circle around it.

Now outside the circle, list out all the things you desire to be true. The more unrealistic it feels, the further on the outside it goes. Don't be shy; this is an opportunity to admit to yourself what you really want.

Everything inside the circle is what you have manifested through your past and current beliefs and frequency.

Everything outside the circle is on another frequency.

We change your frequency by changing your beliefs. The circle gets bigger and bigger to incorporate all those things you desire. We are going to use your wardrobe as a conduit for energy, raising your frequency and bringing those things closer.

Task 2: Argue the case

Draw a line down the middle of a blank piece of paper. One one side, at the top, write your existing money belief. Now write down all the evidence you think you have that affirms this belief, examples you've seen, and other thoughts you have that spin off from here.

Now imagine you are in court, and your job is to argue the other side of the case. Go through each point line by line, and dispute it. Take the time to gather evidence. As we've covered before, your mind is great at deleting information, or interpreting situations to fit its core belief.

Be as objective as possible. If you were presented with the information from the perspective of an observer without the core belief about money, style, and self – what would you conclude? What could also be true about the situation you've described?

Task 3: How are you treating money?

Avoiding your bank balance? Holding your breath in the hope of seeing "approved" every time you tap your card to buy a coffee? Using buy-now-pay-later like it's going out of fashion (it should)? You and money – it's a relationship.

Are you treating this like a respectful, loving, long-term commitment, or like a booty call? Are you being a good friend, or a fuckboy?

Clean out any area of your life relating to money.

Let's start with your purse; the home of your money. If we know the effects of the environment on results, why are we shoving our bank cards into an overstuffed, curled-at-ends, broken-zipped purse, and then expecting more cash?

If you hate your purse, buy a new one you love using. Get rid of any old receipts, lipstick lids, and the fluff hanging around at the bottom of your bags. File your paperwork, don't shove it all into the draw of odd bits and pieces then find yourself in a desperate scramble looking for your account details next time you're on the phone to the car company. Set up standing orders for bills, savings, and investments.

And sure, some of this might sound basic – but are you actually doing it? Roll your eyes all you want; there's a reason you're reading this book.

Chapter 10

Unfix Your Identity

Your identity is not fixed and your wardrobe is one of your most immediate tools for changing it.

In 1999, actor Jim Carrey portrayed comic Andy Kaufman in a biopic called *Man on the Moon*. Carrey is a method actor, an approach that involves deep emotional and psychological immersion into the character he's playing.

Carrey became so immersed in the character of Andy Kaufman that not only did Kaufman's family and friends believe it to be an uncanny portrayal, Carrey lost who Carrey was. In a 2017 interview on the YouTube channel Steve Milne News, Carrey said: 'There is no me, no self. Jim Carrey is gone – actually never existed.'

Said Carrey: 'I realised, "Hey, wait a second. If it's so easy to lose Jim Carrey, who the hell is Jim Carrey?"'[1]

Carrey's experience poses an interesting question about the fluidity of identity.

You only *think* this is your identity because of past experiences, beliefs, and stories. In other words, you are acting out a role – and you get to change the role as and when you choose. That

---

1. *Jim & Andy: The Great Beyond – Featuring a Very Special, Contractually Obligated Mention of Tony Clifton* (2017)

sounds as easy as clicking next on your Spotify playlist. But unfixing your identity is actually hard fucking work.

You've been trained to play a role, based on factors including the culture you live in, the time in which you live, the way you look, and societal expectations.

Identity is front and centre in this book because it underpins all the work we do together. For as long as your identity is fixed, you will continue to get the same results that identity has brought you. I could give you a list of clothes that you "must have" in your wardrobe, but it won't change a thing.

As much as 40 per cent of our daily behaviour is habitual and around 95 per cent of thought happens unconsciously.[2] Let's bring conscious awareness to the beliefs informing your behaviour, which are creating your reality.

Let's say you see yourself as someone who struggles to just about make £2,000 a month. There is too much month left at the end of your money. You believe that money is hard to come by and easy to lose. And on a deeper level, you believe money is the root of all evil; that only bad people can be wealthy. And those who outwardly display the trappings of wealth, such as designer clothes, handbags, or shoes, are stupid and have more money than sense.

You have based your identity on being someone who has up to £2,000 per month and who struggles to get by. This impacts all your decisions, from where you shop right down to your behaviour. You have created an identity that requires £2,000 a month. You have created an identity that requires there to be too much month left at the end of your money.

---

2. Young, E. (2018) *Lifting the lid on the unconscious.* https://www.newscientist.com/article/mg23931880-400-lifting-the-lid-on-the-unconscious/.

So what would happen if you took on a new identity, and decided that you made £50,000 a month easy, that you get to be a good person and a wealthy person, who dresses in high-quality clothes? Your behaviours, actions, and beliefs would have to change.

Person B has a different outlook and approach to life, which results in different outcomes from those of Person A.

As we continue this journey through the wardrobe together, I hope you are able to loosen your grip on what you believe about yourself. I hope you begin to see that your outer reality is a reflection of your inner world.

Which parts of your identity are you willing to examine, change, or improve?

Which beliefs are running on auto-pilot, informing your behaviour and becoming your results?

Which parts of your identity are truly *you* and which parts are constructed through beliefs about who you think you *should* be?

Stop looking at your wardrobe through the lens of who you *think* you are, and begin looking at it through the possibility of who you could be.

That is all there is to it; this book is an examination not of clothes, but of identity.

You are carrying around a metaphorical backpack, with a grip on the straps so tight it's turning your knuckles white. The backpack is called "things I think I am." I hope by the end of this book – or even better, this chapter – you are willing to put it down and leave it here. Or, at the very least, fill it with new stories that support what you really want.

Clothes change your behaviour

One of the most comprehensive studies on identity and clothes concluded that we have three categories of self: **who we hope to be, who we fear we are,** and **who we are most of the time.**[3]

As you go through your wardrobe, consider which categories your clothes fit into and which of those you wear the most. If you wear clothes for the person you hope to be, it's more likely you'll take actions expected of that person.

Enclothed cognition is the term used to describe the link between what we wear and how we behave.

Scientists looked at the differences in behaviour when people wear a doctor's lab coat rather than their own clothes, or a white coat they are told is a painter's smock. They found that when wearing the "doctor's lab coat," participants performed better in tests and had higher attention levels. They concluded there are two necessary factors for the change in behaviour – the symbolism of the item and the wearing of the item.

In other words, to use this psychology for your benefit, the item has to be one you associate with boss mode and you have to actually, ya know... put it on.

You cannot simply buy the dress you dream of wearing one day to deliver a keynote in front of thousands, hang it on the door of your wardrobe, and wait for it to do its magic. You put the dress on now, then you embody the traits of the version of you who walks out on that stage, you act as if you were her and, before you know it, your name is top billing.

---

3. Banim, M., Green, E., Guy, A. (2003) *Through the Wardrobe: Women's Relationships With Their Clothes*. Berg Publishers.

In a separate study on the impact of clothing and behaviour, a professor found that students wearing a Superman logo T-shirt rated themselves as more likeable than peers, and estimated they would be able to physically lift more weight, too.[4]

Next time you get dressed, think less about your choice of outfit as *function*, and more as a tool for behavioural change.

Choose a new story

"That looks great on her, but I could never…"

"She can pull that off, but I can't"

"I'm too [X]."

"I'm not [Y] enough."

A few weeks ago, I went shopping. I picked up a top and skirt co-ord, but instead of trying it on as is I turned the top around to make a waistcoat, layered a shirt underneath, and accessorised. As I emerged from the changing room to talk to my friend, another woman waiting nearby said: 'You must be so confident to do that. I'd love to be able to wear something like that, but I could *never* pull it off.'

Your brain will not make you a liar. It will delete, distort, and generalise information based on your beliefs. Tell yourself that you could never and guess what? You won't.

Words like "never" are definitive, inflexible, and suggest closed-mindedness.

When it comes to style, I hear stories like "I could never" all the time. And the thing with stories? We assume they're based in facts, but there is more than a fair sprinkling of creative licence

---

4. Professor Pine, K. (2014) *Mind What You Wear: The Psychology of Fashion.*

involved. This means we get to re-write them. We can pick a new story that's just as real as the truth we think we've been living.

On speaking further to Ms I Could Never, it emerged that at school, she got bullied for the clothes she wore on non-uniform days. This meant she formed the belief "I'm not stylish." And due to that belief, every experience after was used as affirmative evidence. When she went shopping, she was telling herself: *there is never anything in the shops for me.* Surprise, surprise, she always came away empty-handed and annoyed. When she shopped online, she told herself: *nothing ever fits properly.* Surprise, surprise – the clothes arrived and didn't feel right.

Never (!) mind that as a result of the belief, she did not do her due diligence prior to shopping. There was no planning (the type you'll learn to do in later chapters), no looking at sizing charts. She went to the shops without considering what a good outcome would look like, or how she wanted her clothes to feel, and she shopped online choosing sizes almost at random because not once did she take her measurements, read product descriptions, or consider how these items would fit into her existing wardrobe and for what purpose she was buying them.

Your brain is a pre-programmed computer. You set the parameters of the story and it does whatever it takes to make the information fit. If you've *decided* that everything is against you, the traffic jam you're temporarily waiting in becomes you being stuck in general.

The flat tyre becomes "things happen *to* me, not for me" (forget that you knew the tyre was bald because it barely scraped its last MOT but you did nothing about it). Getting caught in the rain, an unexpected bill, a delayed train… they all become evidence to fit your narrative that indeed, the world *is* against you.

On the same day as occurrences like this, a stranger may have given you a compliment, you received a lovely card in the post, you were told you're getting a pay rise, and your partner cooked you a delicious meal. But you delete that information in favour of your current story.

How much of your behaviour is formed by who you really are… and how much is based on an idea of your identity?

How are your beliefs informing the lens through which you look at your life – and your wardrobe?

How much potential are you wasting by staying in an identity you've been told to wear, like an old jacket or a skirt that doesn't quite fit?

It only takes one

For years and years, it was assumed that a human could not run a mile in four minutes or under. Until one day, Roger Bannister did it. Then, just 46 days later, another runner not only broke the four-minute barrier, he beat Bannister's time. In the year that followed, three more runners broke the four-minute mile. And since then, thousands of runners have followed.

What does this tell you about identity and beliefs?

When you look for evidence that things are possible, they become more likely. You change your behaviour to get the result, because you now see it's possible.

It only takes one. The one gets to be you.

Part Four
The Work

I will never promise instant results, or miracles. But what I can tell you is that the following process is based on years of experience, working with hundreds of women, and if you commit to giving it a go, especially when it feels hard (these exercises are not designed for comfort), things will begin to shift in your relationship with your wardrobe.

This section marks a pivotal moment in our journey together. It was important to give you the context of why you have nothing to wear, and now it's time to do something about it.

For additional tasks and resources to support your journey, visit www.justgetdressed.com.

Chapter 11

The Outfit Diary

You can't change what you can't see: the excuses you make for not doing the work ARE the work.

Bing! Bing!

The sound system played the familiar noise. I was so tired I could barely stop my eyes from closing. But I had to stay alert, because the sound signalled the safety announcement. Whilst others around me were looking at their phones, reading, or already asleep on our many-hours-and-counting-delayed flight, I was paying full attention.

Or rather, I caught myself acting like I was paying full attention. What I was *really* doing was being The Good Girl. The gold-sticker passenger who does as she's told.

This was a habitual pattern I'd been looping all my life… and it was fucking exhausting. I was quite literally – considering this was 3am, I'd been up since 6am the previous day, and this flight was delayed – losing sleep over it. And as this realisation dawned on me, I looked harder at those around me to realise the only other people paying attention were women.

Good girls like me.

We've learned that being "good" means praise. Awarded behaviour included being neat and tidy, listening nicely, being polite, not asking for things you want because that's rude, not sharing your feelings because that's also rude, and putting others above self. Sharing is good, well done. And when little boys are mean or display aggression towards you, it's actually because they like you!

"Bad" behaviour for little girls was, in actuality, the expression of emotions that created problems for the busy adults around us. And this turned us into women who don't want to offend anybody or put them out by being ourselves or asking for what we want.

Despite the cabin crew being paid regardless of who pays attention, and despite that it's our individual responsibility to familiarise ourselves with the safety procedures, it wasn't just how I wanted them to perceive me as the *best passenger ever* that drove my enthusiastic nodding – it was that I wanted to encourage them. I'd not slept for 22 hours at this point, but I fought my body's urge to rest so I could make sure Terry knew I thought they were doing a cracking job.

I'd got to the stage of fatigue where the words of the demonstration were fuzzy. My attention was not for my own benefit, because really I did not have the capacity to take on board new information. And besides, the risk of you being in a plane crash is nearly one in 900 million. And of the plane crashes that do occur, you have a 96 per cent chance of survival.

Being a "good girl" can be fatal

'Do you know where most women die from choking?' asked author Glennon Doyle. 'In the bathroom. We start to choke, then we leave the table so as not to disturb anyone. Then we die, alone, so that we don't disturb the dining folks...

'I teach my children to honor their emotional and physical responses to people, places and ideas.

'When they have to choose between abandoning their own instincts or abandoning some cultural idea of female politeness – I teach them to abandon politeness.'[1]

It's exhausting to constantly try and figure out which version of you is needed in any given moment to a) make other people think of you as "good" and b) meet their needs for validation (our perceived ideas of their need for validation) over your own.

The reality is, Terry could not give a flying fuck if I was nodding along like Churchill the dog. Terry was also exhausted. Terry had spent the last 40 minutes cleaning up other people's shit to get this plane turned around.

It's not that *I* could not give a fuck about you completing this task. I very much give many flying fucks about that. But I must warn you not to dress performatively. Don't be me on a plane. There's no sticker for the girl with the best outfit. There's no gold star for the girl who ticks the boxes for presenteeism. I am uninterested in you putting in loads of extra effort just because you think it will impress me.

What you're really doing when you do that, is repeating a good-girl habit, hiding the truth from yourself, and limiting the result we get from this task. And that would be a shame, because this one exercise is often transformational for clients when they do it right – that is to say, when they're totally honest.

---

1. https://www.facebook.com/glennondoyle/posts/girls-are-trained-to-priori tize-others-comfort-over-our-own-safety-we-are-condit/10157340942024710/

Just Get Dressed

This exercise is designed to bring conscious awareness to unconscious behaviour, before the work has even begun.

If your first reaction to this task is to deny how you actually dress and adjust your style just to match what you think I want – what does that say about you? If your reaction is "cute idea but nope" and then flick over the page – what is that telling you?

Beware your ego. She's a shitty dresser. She'll have you put this book down, fling it across the room, and leave it where it lands under a chest of drawers. You'll discover it again 10 years from now when you're moving house, stressed to the max because you're in the middle of the daunting task of moving all those clothes you've somehow accumulated and never wear.

Well, here I am, your Big Girl Pants in my hand, telling you to put them on and get to work *now*.

I know it feels easier to buy the book, read a few pages, and leave it on the shelf. I know how you fool yourself that you did the work when what you did was answer two of 20 questions. I know how when the book gets brought up in conversation, you say, 'Oh yes! I've read that!' knowing full well you flicked through it and walked away.

This is ego. Saying you read a book you didn't *really* read, is ego. It's you wanting to be seen as a particular version of yourself by others. The cultured, well-read, well-traveled you who exists in another universe somewhere, whilst the version of you here and now watches *Friends* re-runs all Saturday, orange Dorito crumbs all over the sofa.

Think of me as the jumped-up bouncer at the doors of a nightclub called Fabulous Wardrobe. You can hear laughter and happy music inside, disco lights twinkling, everyone's having an amazing time – and your ticket of entry is the dumping of ego.

Tell her you love her, you respect her, you get that she wants to chaperone – but she needs to go home.

The Outfit Diary is the first thing I get my clients to complete. I want to see the diary entries before our first session. Why? You can't change what you can't see.

At this stage, it's likely you *know* you feel a bit rubbish in your clothes, or you've got nothing to wear, or you feel like nothing ever suits you properly. You want to get to feeling stylish, confident, and like dressing is a breeze. But without any awareness of the thoughts, patterns, and beliefs that are informing *how* you dress every day, we can't get from Point A (Nothing to Wear) to Point B (Stylish as Fuck).

I could fill your wardrobe with the most delightful new clothes then come back in six months and you still wouldn't be wearing them. That's because so much of the decision about what to wear is happening without awareness. This task is designed to help you become aware.

It is also designed to mark your progress (as we'll be repeating it a little later) and to help you understand that dressing in a way that makes you feel good has external results. For example, did someone compliment you today? Or did they close the door on you because you looked (and felt) invisible?

Did you feel great and find that the universe conspired to make nice things happen? Or did you roll out of bed two minutes before your meeting, pull on any old thing, feel a bit shit, and have that reflected back to you through the happenings of your day?

Just Get Dressed

Here's how it works:

Every day for the next five days, take a photo of your outfit and answer the questions below.

That's it.

Five minutes a day, yet surprisingly effective. Why? Because you've never asked these questions before. Right now, you know something isn't working. You know something needs to change, but you can't quite put your finger on what. This will help you find it.

- Today I am wearing…
- I decided to wear this because…
- What planning, prep, or thought went into this outfit?
- On a scale of 1-10, with 1 being "troll that lives under a bridge" and 10 being "mediocre white man in middle management" how confident did you feel?
- Positive things that happened today…
- Negative things that happened today…
- How did the way you felt in your outfit impact your reaction(s) to these events?
- If I could improve this outfit in one way, what would it be?

Store this data somewhere safe, as we'll be using it later in our process.

If you're happy to breeze into this exercise, you can go straight to Chapter 12. If you find yourself struggling to do this, the next section is for you.

But I don't own a mirror... and other excuses

"But I don't own a mirror, how can I take photos of my outfits?"

Then go out and buy one. What's going on here is not simply that you don't own a mirror. The practical has become a shield for the emotional and psychological.

If you have found, reading through what was required of you in the Outfit Diary, that your overriding reaction was "no" followed by a litany of excuses seemingly so logical and watertight they'd put a top lawyer to shame, please do the following exercise.

Answer the following (write on the pages, go on, fuck your inner good girl):

Why don't you have a mirror?

YOUR ANSWER HERE:

____

____

And why is that?

YOUR ANSWER HERE:

____

____

And why is that?

YOUR ANSWER HERE:

____

____

Just Get Dressed

And why is that?

YOUR ANSWER HERE:

____

____

You can see that all except the first question were repeats. This is because your first answer is almost never the *real* answer.

As an example, here are the answers of a recent client, shared confidentially but with permission who, like you, did not have a mirror and was using that as a reason not to complete the Outfit Diary.

Why don't you have a mirror? *Because I've not been in my house long and we don't have one.*

Why? *Because I haven't had time to buy one.*

WHY? *Because I'm a mum, I work full-time and I have a lot to do for everyone else.*

Why? *Because I prioritise everyone else over myself.*

Why? *Because I'm not worth spending my time on.*

For another woman, the answers were as follows:

Why don't you have a mirror? *Because I don't like looking at myself.*

Why? *Because I don't like what I see.*

Why? *Because it isn't how I should look?*

Why? *Because I think I've got a big tummy.*

Why? *Because when I was younger my mum used to tell me I needed to lose weight and put me on a diet and she also demonstrated that motherhood equals sacrifice.*

"I don't own a mirror" or any other initial reason you come up with to not do the work, is a surface-level reflection of what is really going on. Reasons like these are ego-driven, and act as protection to avoid shame, accountability, or discomfort.

I have been in hundreds of women's wardrobes and every time I hear "I don't own a mirror" the translation often relates to a childhood memory, which formed a belief, and had implications in their lives reaching further than their wardrobes.

If your lack of a mirror is a manifestation of not believing yourself worthy of having time or resources, it's likely this is evident in all areas of your life.

If the reason you don't want to take photos is because you are uncomfortable with how you look, this likely means you're talking yourself out of all sorts of opportunities in a bid to stay hidden.

I am not here to pressure you into things you're not ready for. This is a workbook, after all, and it takes as long as it takes. But I will tell you a story that reflects the importance, if not the urgency, of doing the work.

Not so long ago, I was invited to a party. I put on my red dress, looked in the mirror… and saw a monster. I tore off the dress and dropped it onto the floor, sobbing. I climbed back into my pyjamas and went to bed. I missed the party.

My now-husband was at the party.

And whilst you could say "what's for you, won't go around you," I missed out on months of potential happiness.

I am sharing this story with you because I need you to understand that when I say *I understand,* I mean it. I know what it's like to wonder why your reflection does not seem to match your inner world. Or to question if what you see is real.

Here are some suggestions – because these are things I have used and done in my own journey.

1. Put Post-it Notes around your mirror with positive words or thoughts about yourself. Your mind will eventually begin to associate those words with the reflection staring back at you.
2. Mirror work (prepare to feel fucking uncomfortable at first): look into your own eyes. Build up to doing this for a minute. If you can only manage 10 seconds at first, that's normal. If you cry, that's normal, too. If words of affirmation come to the surface, speak them.
3. Make getting dressed an event – this will be so much easier when you've been through the wardrobe part of this process. Put on music you love and throw yourself a party. Fuck it, why can't every day be a celebration? Why do we reserve joy, as if it's in short supply, when you get to create it at any moment?

Chapter 12

Your Evolution

You are not who you think you are – and the photographic evidence proves it.

Warning: there may be tears. Please don't rip pages out of this book and use them to wipe your beautiful face. I love you but goddammit do you know how hard I worked on this thing?

Before I explain this task, I think we'd better have another chat about resistance. It is very likely that you will resist this exercise. You'll tell yourself "I don't have time for that" (again), or "I'll come back to that later" (you won't). And then you won't get the results from the work in this book, say it's nonsense, and leave me a shitty Amazon review. Don't do that to me. Don't do it to yourself.

Just get the fucking work done, so we can go ahead and just get dressed.

Resistance is extremely common when it comes to wardrobes. We don't want to feel the potential guilt or shame that arises when we have to turn and face into the piles of clothes we never wore, or the ones we've been driving around with inside the boot of our cars for the past six months (yes, I see you).

If we don't do this work, then we don't have to make a decision on what to do with that jumper we hate, but feel we can't get rid of, because our sister passed it onto us. When you keep hold of a jumper, dress, or holey pair of tights you hate because your friend no longer wants it, good-girl conditioning is running wild with your wardrobe.

You think it makes you a bad person to reject your sister's off-cuts, but what right did she have to pass it on to you? Did she ask your permission to pass it on and wait for a full-bodied yes or no? Or did she *inform* you that you were taking it off her hands? Do you feel that you are able to share your true thoughts and feelings with the person who uses you as their metaphorical reject pile?

She may not be your sister; it could be your mother, a friend, or a colleague.

In almost every wardrobe I've ever been inside, there are items passed over that go unworn and unloved, carrying a heavy energy of guilt and shame because the new owner thinks getting rid of it means they are somehow rejecting the former owner.

It isn't fair for someone to burden you with the guilt they refuse to carry, whether intentional or otherwise. If they bought a top they never wore, the answer isn't "dump it on [Jessica] and let her deal with it." It is not your responsibility to find space – physically or emotionally – so someone else doesn't have to face their decisions.

This exercise is about facing *your* decisions, and I'd like you to do it with as little self-judgement as possible. What's done is done, you can't change the past. But you can have a different relationship with your wardrobe in the future.

Don't resist. Go there. Into every nook, cranny and spider-dwelling corner.

Go boldly into your wardrobe

In this task, we are going to chart your style journey, or evolution, if that feels like a word you can legitimately use for it.

The reason I love this exercise is it's very hard to argue with photographic evidence. Here inside this pretty little head of yours (women, huh, so fragile!) you've made yourself out to be this terrible failure of a human who has achieved nothing, has done nothing but go backwards in terms of her appearance, and who needs to keep spending her life chasing what she thought she once had (but ironically at the time she thinks she had it, did nothing but berate herself for not being good enough).

But when you look back at photos of yourself, they remind you of all the things you conveniently forgot for the sake of affirming your (incorrect) beliefs.

You'll remember how much you've grown in confidence. All the things you learned. How strong you were for handling particular situations. How determined you've been to get to here from where you once were. How you beat the odds. How you loved so fiercely, lost, grieved, loved again, gave your all, started over with nothing, were generous with your time, your skills, your empathy. The places you went to, the experiences you've had. The things that made you laugh, smile, and cry. You have lived and instead of calling it living – you've called it "not enough." You've compared your brilliant, messy, full of joy, anger, frustration, beauty, love, and wonderful life with some shit you saw on Instagram.

You will likely find images you want to keep out, put on your desk, your mirror, and in your purse, to remind you how amazing you are.

Just Get Dressed

You decided you've achieved nothing, except trying to lose the same 10lbs over and over again – but *here* is the evidence this is untrue.

Surviving in the fuckfest we call modern society in an era of megalomaniacs, billionaires with bad intentions, patriarchal standards, and AI bots that are hoodwinking decent people, famines, wars, climate change, and a million-and-one-things on your to-do list, is a big win on its own.

And as well as doing that, you've actually managed some pretty awesome achievements. But you shrug off compliments, feedback, and genuine respect for your work because "it's nothing."

It's fucking *everything*, actually.

And if you owned how much it really was, wow – what a world we could create.

The first time I did this task, it covered 10 years. The next time it was one year – and now I am doing six months. Why? Firstly, because I do not have any photos from before that 10-year period. One or two here or there, where mostly I'm hiding in the background or smiling awkwardly because I hated having my photo taken.

There was a time, before I did all the work I'm giving you inside this book, when I literally could not bear to look at photos of myself. My lovely nan made me a book of images for some birthday or another, and I actually tore out the pages and threw them away. You might be reading this, open-mouthed at my… lack of gratitude? My attitude?

You might judge me for that. You might think I've been mean, selfish, unappreciative. Yes, I was all those things. And I was also suffering. I could not bear to look at those photos, because they evoked all the pain of that girl.

Now, thank you to the work inside this book – over a sustained period of time I must add – I do regret my decision. But I don't blame myself for it. It was all part of a necessary process, so that I can sit here, telling you this story today.

The more effort you put into your style confidence journey, the quicker your evolutions will happen. My style will not be quite the same when this book is published and in your lovely hands, as it was when I was writing it. How exciting is that?

Just Get Dressed: End of chapter task

Collect several images of yourself from the specified time-frame. If this is your first time doing this task, I'd suggest going for a period of time over which your life has changed. For example, if you used to work in a corporate role, and now you run a business, take your first photo from back in your office days.

Or if you have children, you could choose before and after.

Or perhaps something significant happened in your life within the past few years that has shaped who you are today.

Look back at how your style has evolved, and what it says about where you were at this specific moment in time.

Answer the following questions:

- In what ways am I stronger, more resilient, sharper, more evolved, and more confident now?
- What has changed about my style since then?
- What can I appreciate about these past versions of me?

Just Get Dressed

- If I could go back in time and talk to myself then, what would I tell that person?
- What would she tell me?
- If I imagine where I am now as the starting point, and where I'll be five years from now as the after, what will have changed? Who will I have become?

Now list out 3-5 things you'll take forward into your style from here.

Part Five
Your New Style Vision

Style was always yours to define and now it's time to actually do it.

Let's do away with any resistance to the idea that you want to be stylish. You are *allowed* to be stylish. Hell, you're allowed to paint yourself green and ask everyone to refer to you as a Swamp Monster if you want to. There really are no rules.

No really – *there are no rules*. Personal style is whatever *you* decide.

The dictionary definition of style in this context is "a distinctive appearance, typically determined by the principles according to which something is designed." This suggests that rather than style being about conformity – ironically the thing you've been dressing for your entire life – it's about *individuality*.

If you want to free yourself from the burden that there is a defined version of style you'll never reach, you should probably know that style never meant what you thought it does. The word style derives from the Latin *stylus* which was a small pointed writing instrument.[1] Since people would use this tool to express themselves, in one sense *style* simply means self-expression.

We've looked at the influences on how you're currently dressing and have dressed in the past, and now we're going to seek new influences for the future. But it's important to remember you're looking for *inspiration*, not paint-by-numbers. You're learning to listen to, and trust, your inner style guidance system, not making a list of what to go out and buy to look exactly like Woman You Think Is Stylish.

So before we go any further, it's time for you to make your own definition of what style means to you.

- What would it look like if you were able to define yourself as stylish?
- If you were standing in front of a mirror in the most stylish outfit you could think of, what would you see?
- What are the habits of the kind of woman you define as stylish? What are her beliefs? What does her wardrobe look like?
- Who are the real-life women or people (or characters from TV and film) whose style you admire? Why?
- If you could swap wardrobes with anyone (someone you know in real life, a celebrity or character from TV, film or a book) – who would it be? Why?
- Get honest again – as you're doing this work, what beliefs are coming up about why you can't/don't/won't?

---

1. *Style - Etymology, origin & Meaning* (no date). https://www.etymonline.com/word/style.

Chapter 13

Who Do You Want to Be?

Decide who you want to become, dress as her now, and tell someone about it.

If clothes are a costume you can wear to change your identity, who do you want to dress as today?

Now you understand why your wardrobe isn't working, let's delve into the psychology and energetics of clothing. By the end of this chapter, you'll see you have the power to believe something new about yourself and create your outfits accordingly.

How exciting to be on the precipice of a style evolution.

In the following chapters, I will guide you through the process. It will require time, determination, and courage. It will ask you to delve into dark corners and uncover long-forgotten items and beliefs. It will need your commitment not to walk away, or shame yourself. And it will require your re-commitment every day, sometimes multiple times a day, to the vision we are about to create.

Every journey starts with direction. If I asked you to get into a car and drive, we'd pootle around aimlessly, probably end up down a one-way street or going round and round the orbital. Deciding where you're going is a fundamental part of the process – how the hell do we know how to dress, if we don't know what we're trying to manifest? Lack of clarity or direction is one of the key reasons we do not achieve (or even set) goals.

You're a grown fucking woman, so you won't be getting a template from me of exactly how to set your goals or what they are. You don't need me to tell you what you want; you need to learn (how many times have I said this already) to *trust yourself.*

You know what you want. No, stop that – you really do.

"I don't know what I want" has become code for "I'm scared to admit what I want."

Why? Because maybe it means blowing up your current life. Maybe it means discomfort for others. Maybe it will mean being called selfish, stupid, bad. Maybe it's because your entire life has been about conformity.

> *By age {x} you should have {y} and so what, you're unhappy?! Nobody's really happy! Anyone who says they are is lying! No one ever really gets what they want. Life is a series of compromises and battling to keep just one of two pieces of enjoyment to brighten up the days.*

Maybe you're scared of failure? The perceived embarrassment of saying what you want and it not coming true? If anything is proof you have the power to make your dreams come true, let it be this book.

I was an eccentric little girl. I always had my head in a book, or I was writing a story. I loved learning facts so I could say to my dad, 'Did you know [this random thing about grasshoppers]?'

I used clothes as a way to try on different personalities, and a very important consideration before I took on any imaginary role was always the costuming. I'd have imaginary conversations with my costume department, like I was running a Netflix show in my own head decades before Netflix became a thing.

We didn't have very much money, but my mum was pretty good at indulging my imagination, and she was artistic. She would make costumes for me out of whatever was laying around the house. I bet if I saw those costumes now, I'd think "that's a plastic bag and some bottle tops" but at the time it felt magical. She allowed me to live in a world of my imagination, which became increasingly better, as time went on, than the reality in which I lived.

One day, I came across a woman's business briefcase-style bag. I had to have it. It was mock (at least I hope mock) croc skin, royal blue, with a yellow leaf pattern on the satin material in the front. What's a school-age kid from a council estate doing with a woman's business briefcase, you might ask? This kid was playing a game of imagination, in which she was a 30-something -year-old author.

I had no comprehension at the time that what I was doing was manifesting. But somewhere on my timelines, was a 30-something-year-old version of me who'd written a book. Maybe several books. Maybe the version of myself I saw is one that doesn't exist yet. Maybe she's who I become five years from now.

I could see my books so clearly sitting there inside that briefcase, the pages not yet filled, the subject matter not yet defined – but I knew they were there nonetheless. It took a couple of decades – the majority of which I spent convinced by the world that my secret dream of becoming an author was unrealistic – but here I am today, just a few chapters away from finishing my first book.

I no longer have that briefcase, but I never lost the dream. That briefcase, and the little girl who carried it, still live on. She manifested me into reality, without any understanding that's what she had done. It was like she wasn't imagining; she had an ability to look into the future when she was looking into that bag.

I hope this story demonstrates not only the power of your dreams and why you should never give up on them, but also the power of clothes in helping you make them happen.

Yes it's taken 20-something years, but if you can see it, imagine it, taste it – there's a reason. If there is something that's felt like your destiny for the longest time – there's a reason. That thing you've always secretly dreamed of achieving – the book you haven't penned, the song you never sung, the adventure you never went on – is somewhere out there on your timeline. The only reason it hasn't happened yet is because you do not have the identity of the woman for whom it's real. You know she is capable of existing, because you already created her somewhere, whether in your mind or in some liminal space we can not access or see. Now is the time to dress her into being.

You may get knocked from the path sometimes. You may fall into the trap of believing it's unrealistic, or too late, or not something "somebody like you" could ever achieve. Keep believing anyway. Get back on the path. Honour that little girl who bought herself the briefcase to carry her published books.

And that's what we're doing with your wardrobe – your outfits are the tool you use to step, literally and figuratively, into the shoes of the women you always wanted to be.

Don't rush the process

I know you have an urge to take everything out of your wardrobe and throw it dramatically from the windows whilst shouting, 'See you in hell, terrible jeans that never fit and made me feel like shit about myself for years!'

Love that for you (though your neighbours won't).

But nothing permanent was ever made in haste. It has taken years of repeated messaging to make you feel like you can't/won't/don't. So it's going to take more than a Pinterest board and a double-shot of espresso to create a vision so powerful, it lasts.

The chances are (unless you're a client of mine), you won't have been through a process like this before, and envisioning this next-level identity, or thinking in intricate detail about the habits, beliefs, and outfits you'll have is not something you're used to.

If at first your answers to the questions in this section are "I don't know" be sure to add "yet" – and be sure to keep coming back to them, within these pages or in your mind. Lasting change doesn't come from doing something one time – it's repetitive, and often mundane. It's re-committing every day to the vision, and getting back on the path when things knock you off.

You're not too old, and it's not too late

That's unrealistic. I'm too old to do that. It's too late for me, I've missed my chance. I could never wear this.

Stop stop stop stop juststopitnowplease. "It's too late" or "you should desperately try to regain your youth" is nothing more than a marketing campaign by companies selling you faux-miracle products.

In 2008, Rush Limbaugh said of Hillary Clinton: "Will this country want to actually watch a woman get older before their eyes on a daily basis?"

Wrote Julie Daley for HuffPost: "With a masterful stroke of the mouth, he attempted to disempower this woman by using one of the patriarchy's greatest weapons, the deeply held belief that age makes women ugly, worthless and powerless."[1]

Here's the thing about patriarchy: we've been living it for centuries, but it doesn't make it anywhere near as old as the cultures and religions that once, or still do, revere older women. The elderly lady in Buddhism symbolises a determined seeker of wisdom and enlightenment.[2] In Hindu traditions, elderly ladies are revered for their experience and wisdom.[3] In Celtic mythology, "hag" is a title for the divine figure known as the Cailleach, a powerful goddess of winter and the land.[4]

As I write, we have closed out the final chapter on the tale of Carrie Bradshaw, with the *Sex and the City* spin-off *And Just Like That* coming to an end after three seasons. Sarah Jessica Parker is in her 60s. During the second-to-last episode of the much-critiqued (mostly by me, a loyal hate-watcher who sticks through

---

1. Daley, J. (2011) 'Old woman, wise woman, powerful woman: The beauty of aging,' *HuffPost*, 17 November. https://www.huffpost.com/entry/old-woman-wise-woman-powe_b_798942.
2. Le, H.A.T. (2020) 'Buddhist way of old age and women's life course in Ho Chi Minh City (Vietnam),' *The Australian Journal of Anthropology*, 31(3), pp. 319–332. https://doi.org/10.1111/taja.12373.
3. Pandya, S. (2016) 'Hindu women in religious orders: Understanding their well-being in old age.' *Journal of Religion Spirituality & Aging* 28(3):1-20.
4. Blackie, S. (2022) *Hagitude: Reimagining the Second Half of Life*. New World Library.

the mundanity and often pointless plotlines of the new series because of how much I loved the original), Carrie was carrying a Coach oversized clutch bag. I have a contact who designs such bags. The entire line – which had been on the website for months prior – sold out within a weekend.

Older women have influence. Don't let the fact that a beauty company hired a 17-year-old to sell anti-ageing skincare products make you forget this. It's nothing but patronisation. The lie that it's too late, or that no one will take you seriously as you mature, or that you can't be a style icon as you age, are fabrications designed to stop you from *doing the thing*. Because imagine how dangerous midlife women could be if they put down the baggage and picked up the pen.

One study shows that older entrepreneurs outperform younger peers, up to the age of 60.[5] Vera Wang launched her namesake fashion house at age 40, and has since dressed the likes of Victoria Beckham and Mariah Carey.[6] And besides, in the grand passage of time, you are but a nanosecond. A snap of fingers. A blink of an eye.

To quote the late and iconic Catherine O'Hara as Moira Rose:

> "Take a thousand naked pictures of yourself now. You may currently think, 'Oh, I'm too spooky,' or, 'Nobody wants to see these tiny boobies.' But believe me, one day

---

5. Mehta, K. (2022) *Older entrepreneurs outperform younger Founders—Shattering ageism.* https://www.forbes.com/sites/kmehta/2022/08/23/older-entrepre neurs-outperform-younger-foundersshattering-ageism/.
6. Luu, C. (2025) *Expect to 'age out' of your career, says Vera Wang - she's had at least four.* https://www.bbc.co.uk/culture/article/20250304-vera-wang-influential-interview-katty-kay.

> you will look at those photos, with much kinder eyes and say, 'Dear God, I was a beautiful thing!'"[7]

Here's your next task:

Imagine you are 100 years old. Think about the life you've had, the things you're proud of, and what you wished you didn't spend so much time worrying about. Write a letter to yourself today, from a 100-year-old you.

What words of wisdom does she have for you? What does she want you to know? What would she tell you to stop, or start doing? Who or what is she grateful to have in her life? What does she know about the path you're on, or the results of your current actions if you continue with them?

Sometimes it helps to zoom out of your everyday, where your belly and thighs feel like the biggest hurdle in the world, and gain some perspective about what life is really about.

Once you've written this letter, I want you to contemplate what it would be like to never become that 100-year-old you. Imagine if today was your last day on this earth. At 30 years old, or 40, or 50, being 100 feels so far away you think you have plenty of time. Yet time is the one thing none of us are guaranteed. You can make more money, you can change your appearance, you can move to a new country and start a new life, but that life has a time limit – so why waste a second of it?

---

7. *Schitt's Creek*, Season 5, episode 14, 'Life is a Cabaret', Eugene Levy and Dan Levy, CBC.

Think bigger

Thinking bigger forces you to change at fundamental levels, in a way incremental goals do not. You would dress vastly differently, both in terms of the effort you put in and the quality of what you wear, if you thought of yourself as someone who makes 10 times the money you do now. Or as the author of multiple best-selling books. Or the Prime Minister. Or whatever your dream job, bank balance, and life looks like.

What you think is who you become, not the other way around.

Be → do → have.

Not have → do → be.

Let's say your goal is to make an additional £100 per month. It would take a little effort, but not fundamental changes. Making or even saving £100 per month could look like shopping around for your groceries, cancelling a few subscriptions, or selling some unwanted clothes (you'll likely have a few after our closet clean-out) on Vinted.

Now let's say your goal is to make an additional £10,000 per month. You're instantly forced to think on a whole other level. Someone who makes an additional £10,000 per month has a different identity than your current one. Firstly, they have to believe it is possible to make an additional £10,000 per month. And then they have to behave at the level of someone who's making that money.

If you're reading this on the 10th day of the month, and I tell you that you have until the 30th to generate an additional £10,000, there are habits and behaviours you'd instantly quit. No more procrastination, no more downplaying or undercharging. Maybe you'd finally demand that pay rise we both know is long overdue, or put your prices up. And in doing so, you'd have to change your identity.

Now let's say your goal is to make an additional £100,000 per month. Who would you have to be if you were making that happen? Which habits, behaviours, outfits, relationships, and parts of your environment would have to immediately change?

You don't realise that you're currently competing to be mediocre, because most people are thinking small. Most people are thinking incremental wins.

"Ninety-nine per cent of people in the world are convinced they are incapable of achieving great things, so they aim for mediocre," Tim Ferris once wrote. "The level of competition is thus fiercest for 'realistic' goals, paradoxically making them the most time and energy-consuming."[8]

The point of what we're doing isn't to get to the goal – it's to become the version of ourselves for whom the goal is a real possibility.

Get witnessed

People who set clear and measurable goals are 76 per cent more likely to reach them than those who don't. And further research finds those who write their goals down are 42 per cent more likely to achieve them. But being witnessed? That's where the true magic is.

James Donaldson, aka MrBeast, is a YouTube creator who has

---

8. Ferriss, T. (2007) *The 4-Hour work week: Escape 9-5, Live Anywhere, and Join the New Rich*. Crown.

amassed millions of followers and millions of pounds.[9] I'm using him as a case study here, not just because hearing this story had a profound effect on the way I set goals for myself, but also because MrBeast is a philanthropist and has done lots of good with the money he's made. And you know by now, we need more money in the hands of good people – like you – so that we can address some of this *gestures vaguely* general fuckery.

As a teenager, MrBeast set himself an audacious goal for his YouTube channel. But rather than leaving it in the notes app of his phone, he created videos set for a specific date in the future. In 2015 he recorded a video titled "Hi Me In 5 Years." He scheduled the video to publish exactly five years later. He only had about 9,000 subscribers at the time, but he told his future self in the video that he expected he would have one million subscribers by 2020.

By 2020 he had more than 50 million subscribers. In five years, he had become one of the largest YouTubers in the world.[10]

Knowing that video was going live on a set date, to be witnessed by the world, pushed him to go for it.

After I read about Mr Beast, I decided to employ the same tactic. I told my community, on December 31, that in 2025 I was going to make £50,000 per month. This was 150 per cent more than my highest previous sales month. By June 30, 2025, I had achieved the goal. Forcing myself to be witnessed also forced me to instantly step into the identity of the woman who achieved them. I had to look at my habits, behaviours, patterns, and outfits and ask: would I [do this, be this, wear this] if I was [at my goal]?

---

9. My First Million (2025) *MrBeast isn't cute. Here's his brutal business lessons.* https://www.youtube.com/watch?v=eFKLymJpZS8.
10. MrBeast (2020) *Hi me in 5 years.* https://www.youtube.com/watch?v=AKJfak Esgy0.

If you're worried people in your life will think you're delusional, or will piss all over your dreams no sooner than you've told them – send me an email at samantha@thestyleeditor.co.uk and tell me what they are instead.

What's worse?

Is it more embarrassing to unapologetically go after what you want, or to allow the opinions of others (or your perception of their opinions) stop you?

A few years ago, a "friend" came across one of my notebooks, in which I'd written quotes I found inspirational from notable women. She sent it around the WhatsApp groups, I assume in a bid to mock me.

It's embarrassing, isn't it? Being someone who has goals. Much cooler to conform. To pretend you don't care about anything. To sit by and watch other people achieve *your* dreams; feel the sharp pang of envy in your chest as they share updates and celebrations. Whilst the fear of failure is one of the biggest reasons not to set goals, I bet one of your reasons is that people might find out.

Picture the celebrity, author, artist, or business woman you most admire. Do you see her as someone who has goals, or who doesn't? Is she ambitious, or not?

She would not be in the Netflix show, have penned best-sellers, have written the finest works of music that you get to watch, read, or hear without telling people of her ambition. She didn't write the manuscript, then think: 'Let me hide that in the drawer where no one else will ever read it until I die and some great-niece is clearing out my possessions, opens the drawer, and finds the yellowing, curled-cornered, dust-covered document.'

She had to risk ridicule, criticism and rejection to get that content into your hands. What are you willing to risk to become who you really want to be?

This isn't one and done

Reaching new levels means understanding there is no peak to the mountain. You're scaling to new ledges, but never reaching the summit. You will have to come back to this workbook over and over again, because your style is going to evolve as your life, bank account, and personality does.

My advice? Just get over it. The universe is in a state of expansion, you are part of the universe – your one job is to evolve and expand, so you can resist all you like and come up with reason after reason why now is not the time. Or you can accept that no sooner than you've evolved your style through this first go round, things will begin to shift in your life, and it will be time to do this all over again.

Being here is a commitment to your continual evolution. There are many versions of yourself you are yet to meet, and they're all waiting for you on this journey. Imagine who you'll be next time you come back to these exercises, and the next. How exciting to think you are on the precipice of evolution that will take you to incredible places, all through your wardrobe.

Chapter 14

Seeing is Believing

Your wardrobe is a business decision, and when you outgrow who you were, your clothes need to catch up.

Now you've put some thoughts to your new style direction, it's time to bring it to life through visuals. One in five successful entrepreneurs uses vision boards, and over 80 per cent say their business is aligning with the things they desired.[1]

Neuroscientist Dr Tara Swart explains in an article that "looking at images on a vision board primes the brain to grasp opportunities that may otherwise have gone unnoticed. That's because the brain has a process called 'value-tagging' which imprints important things onto your subconscious and filters out unnecessary information."

She goes further into explaining that "the brain assigns a higher 'value' to images than written words on a to-do list." The more you look at those images, the more those images increase in value. This phenomenon is known as the Tetris Effect.[2]

1. Bank, T. (2018) *Visualizing goals influences financial health and happiness, study finds.* https://www.prnewswire.com/news-releases/visualizing-goals-influences-financial-health-and-happiness-study-finds-300207028.html.
2. Pham, S. (2024) 'Science Behind Vision Boards,' *Medium.* https://medium.com/@sashadomenech/science-behind-vision-boards-efb4dd229441

I use visual boards in my work so my clients can more easily understand the idea I have in my mind about the direction for their style. Without doing this piece of the work, we are dressing blind. Shopping with no direction, accumulating stuff with little thought. Back to square one no sooner than the tags have come off the clothes. So now it's time to take your ideas and bring them together with visual references.

You can use whichever media feels best for you – cut and stick images from magazines, create a Pinterest board, or find images to print out and pin. You could use an app like Canva and pull in images, graphics, and colours. You could even describe (in lots of detail) your vision to an AI tool and have it create a visual for you.

What's your vision?

Don't think too much about what you collect, stick, and paste or add to your board. This is an opportunity to let the creative parts of you that were quashed under the expectation of "sensibility" run wild once again. And if you are thinking 'I don't do creativity,' this is an opportunity for you to get out of your comfort zone.

We're focusing on style for this exercise, but you can create vision boards for any of your goals. I use them for business branding, business goals, health and wellbeing, talks, personal brand and yes, even the design of this book.

The important thing is seeing it, not making it on January 1 with all the promise of a new year, shoving it in a drawer, and finding it eleven months later – then using it as yet another reason to call yourself a failure.

How you do this process is up to you, but the way I get the best results from my vision board is by adding images to my phone and laptop as a screensaver. Whilst you aren't consciously registering what you see every time you open your phone (many more times a day than you think), repetitively seeing the images will make a difference.

In December, I created my vision board for the year and set it as the wallpaper on my phone.

As I write this, eight months into the year, everything I put on the board has come true. Except for one thing: best-selling book (but we are working on that!)

Your style vision board can contain images, wording, colours, textures – whatever feels right.

Take your time and don't settle.

Part Six

This is Not a
Closet Clean-Out

Your wardrobe is a living thing, not a museum. Give yourself permission to engage with it.

It looked great. Clashing colours, texture, stompy heels that meant you couldn't miss me... But it felt awful. Too small, but not physically – I'd outgrown it, but not through my size. Technically, it still *fit*. But in the ways that mattered, it didn't.

I was on my way to an important meeting in Spring, 2024. Living just minutes from a train station is very handy when you like to wear shoes other people deem ridiculous, and so the obligatory pair of bright boots was on. I did my usual Instagram story post (gotta give the fans what they want) and received all the heart-eye emojis and "looking fab!"s. I didn't feel it though. And this was a problem.

On the train, I mentally scanned through the look. Shoes, skirt, blouse, jacke– *the skirt!* Despite its gorgeous glimmering magenta, this was a skirt almost as old as me. And that wouldn't normally be a problem, except for the quality. It was old but not in a quality vintage way. It was old in a came-from-a-high-street-fast-fashion-store way and felt as static as a plastic bag against my legs (and likely made from the same material).

Then it hit me: I've outgrown my wardrobe. I can't keep wearing the same items in the same way and expect different results.

Yes, it's good to feel comfortable in your clothes (I hate the idea that you can't be comfortable and stylish, people often tell me this like it's definitive when I know it is not) but on an energetic level, your clothes should feel stretchy. Clothes are not merely items. They're a result, like you, of energy; they have the ability to raise your frequency, change your psychological state, therefore your actions and, ultimately, your results.

So much had happened in my life since acquiring this skirt, I did not feel like the same person who bought it.

I can be candid enough here, given all we've shared, to admit that what I did next was a bad decision borne of my lack of foresight. Had I paid attention to the signs it was time for a wardrobe upgrade – feeling slightly sticky in business, less-than-ideal clients, a slow sales month – I would have got this sorted before the morning of my big meeting. But alas, there we were on the 8.13am into Paddington for a 9.30am meeting.

I knew I could not face the meeting in this energy; so I dived into a boutique I've visited a number of times and, with the help of the wonderful shop assistant, quickly selected a dress.

Much better. Meeting went well.

And I learned an extremely valuable lesson: *listen to your energy and schedule your wardrobe audits.*

If you take one thing from the entirety of this book, let it be this – what you wear is a business decision and booking days into your diary to sort out your wardrobe is on company time. I don't give a fuck what your boss says. See what he says when you rock up next week in an Oodie because you're out of outfit ideas, are done with the pressure of choosing what to wear every day, and can no longer be bothered. Yeah, he'd soon recognise why what you wear is a business problem – there is no way he's putting you in front of a client like this.

If you run your own business, don't let your inner pale, stale, male boss take over. This is not you being selfish. This is not wasted time. It's a business investment and must be treated as such.

I'm no stranger to a closet clean-out. Up to the point of my GTR (Great Train Realisation), I'd performed dozens of them with clients.

But this was different – it was a ritual. I got home that day, pulled everything out of my wardrobe, and made a decision about who I wanted to be. This is the ritual I'm going to guide you through, and I can confidently say it changed my life. In the month that followed this experience, and thanks to making the decision to become this next version of myself and dress like her, I doubled my sales. And every time I have done this since, I've experienced the same, or an equally incredible result.

Stop scrolling through Instagram hoping you catch success through the screen. The answer is not *out there*. It is likely inches away from where you are currently sitting. It's inside your wardrobe.

Put your favourite music on, put down your phone, and step inside.

Chapter 15

Wardrobe Reality Check

Playing dress-up is a legitimate business activity.

Now that you have your style vision, your moodboard, and inspirational references, we are going to look at how much of your wardrobe matches it. We are going to find the weak links, make a list of missing pieces, and create new outfits that reflect who you want to be – but which are practical enough for you to actually wear them.

When was the last time you removed everything from your wardrobe?

The last time you moved? Last winter? When you got a new job?.... Never?[1]

I'm not talking about a seasonal sort, or a "keep, toss, donate" Sunday afternoon, upcoming- event-and-nothing-to-wear-induced panic.

Your wardrobe is a living thing – it is not a museum. Yet most people stuff theirs full like a display cabinet to which they've lost the keys. They do surface-level housekeeping; a move about here, a change-over-the-hangers there. But getting everything out and processing what it means? Don't be stupid. Almost as stupid as reading a book about clothes, amiright?

------

1. Come on, we both know the answer is "never."

161

If your clothing represents your *identity*, then surely the place you house that identity should be less "dark wooden box gathering dust" and more "shrine to your highest potential"?

Your wardrobe may well currently be a place of frustration and stress, for many or any of the reasons we've covered. But the fact you can't open it properly because the hinge has been broken for the last two years, the mirror is cracked, or it's so full you'd rather run naked through the streets yelling 'I've got nothing to wear!' than go there, will, in part at least, be adding to the problem.

If, throughout this book, you've felt a sense of confusion about your identity, if the questions around your vision leave you clueless, this likely correlates to how shut off you are from your relationship with your wardrobe.

A wardrobe is, after all, a representation of self.

When someone asks 'Who are you?' you list all the ways you mean something to other people. Wife, mother, football coach, service-provider, C-suite executive, volunteer. This tells them what you *do* – it doesn't tell them who you *are*. What do you think you're on this planet at this time for? That's what I'm really asking when *I* asked, 'Who are you?'

Let go of the guilt

This process is not yet another excuse to give yourself a hard time. Women already have enough guilt to contend with. It's like from the minute you're born, you're popped into a babygrow with an invisible cloak of shame.

Anything from your body (we still don't teach girls the proper names for their body parts and then wonder why they feel disconnected from themselves), to the way you speak, look, what you eat, how you walk, how you stand and sit ("that's not very ladylike"), the interests you have, how neat you are, your handwriting, how well you get along and play nice… are monitored constantly.

And let's not forget, you're likely from a generation where hitting kids for being naughty was totally normal, so your nervous system learned to contract and brace whenever you do something "wrong." And for you, as a woman, something wrong often means simply existing.

Sometimes a client will express a feeling of inadequacy because she forgot about the items lurking down the back of her wardrobe. I'll get her to list out all the responsibilities she has in life. Her business/job, her children, her marriage, her parents, siblings, friendships, the housework, her community (online and IRL). And on top of all of that, she is expecting herself to somehow keep a running inventory in her head of every item in her wardrobe.

Girl, I love you, but you're not a fucking iPhone. You don't exist to make lists. Your beautiful brain is already storing way too much information, and simultaneously being bombarded with *more* information – you really think you also have an extra 100 Megabytes of internal storage for this?

Life is not the same as it was for your granny. She only has five dresses, a sweater, and a raincoat and somehow you're making that mean *you* should have less. And whilst we'll absolutely be getting into the scourge of fast fashion, overconsumption, and the role we play – your life and grandma's are in no way the same. Comparing the closet of a woman from 2026 to that of a woman from 1956 is like comparing an Apple watch and a typewriter.

I would never suggest granny had it easy, or diminish her experiences, but please consider the context in which you are living before you start with the self-inflicted guilt trip of having too many clothes. In the 1950s, likely your gran was a stay-at-home mother whose job was running a household (a fulltimefuckingjobjustfyi).

Today, your job is your *job*, plus you're the head of the PTA, you're responsible for the household, you've got technology that keeps you in touch with a much wider network than granny had, you have access to finances in a way she didn't. Granny was required to be housekeeper and maybe "woman at party" one or two evenings a week.

You are required to be cleaner, executive at a law firm, head of the PTA, social media and brand manager, internet and real-life friend, taxi driver, courier, event attendee, event organiser, event speaker, podcast producer and host, admin clerk for self and entire family, IT department, nighttime attendant for children who won't sleep even though you need to be up at 5am for work, and sometimes "woman at party."

GIVE. YOURSELF. A. FUCKING. BREAK.

This modern lifestyle means multiple roles, which means multiple outfits. We as a *collective* have an issue with overconsumption, and you as an *individual* have an insanely busy schedule requiring three times the clothing your grandmother needed.

Psychotherapist Nancy Colier says women's propensity for guilt is both biological and socially learned.[2] Whilst our "empathetic

---

2. Rev, N.C.L. (2022) 'If something is wrong, it doesn't mean it's your fault.,' *Psychology Today*, 12 October. https://www.psychologytoday.com/gb/blog/inviting-monkey-tea/202210/the-guilt-women-suffer.

wiring isn't the problem {...} we turn this beautiful quality, with which we're gifted, into the self-destructive habit called guilt." In one study, women listed more reasons than men for why they feel guilty, both in their personal and professional lives.[3]

Says Colier: "At the same time, through our cultural conditioning, we've learned we can best achieve emotional safety and belonging by being likeable."

"Likeable" for many of the women I work with has become synonymous with hating oneself. Self-deprecation is shorthand for "be my friend, I'm no threat" because we've all been primed to compete with each other for a relatively small pool of opportunities and money, when we could be working together for more.

Guilt coupled with the need for likeability are big blockers to improving your style. Guilt keeps you in avoidance; you can tell yourself the reason you never do this is "I don't have time," but really you don't want to confront the parts of yourself staring back at you in your closet.

Needing to be likeable keeps your style experimentation just the right side of the invisible line between "she's unbothersome" and "fucking bitch."

Which leads us onto the next question...

---

3. Luck, T. and Luck-Sikorski, C. (2022) 'The wide variety of reasons for feeling guilty in adults: findings from a large cross-sectional web-based survey,' *BMC Psychology*, 10(1), p. 198. https://doi.org/10.1186/s40359-022-00908-3.

When was the last time you played dress up?

When you were five? When you had an event to go to, no idea what to wear, and spent a feverish Friday night screaming in your Spanx as you desperately tried all sorts of combinations? *Never?* Maybe the feverish Friday nights are too much for you to bear, so you simply buy a new outfit (or five, none of which you end up wearing) for every event.

We can't possibly ring-fence the time to play dress-up. We've got so much work to do, emails to send, packed lunches to make, dogs to walk, ironing to sort, birthday cards to buy, bills to pay, cleaning to do, plants to water. We're wives, mothers, sisters, daughters, and friends *first*, human beings deserving of good things *second. Or maybe not at all.*

The guilt you feel about potentially taking a few hours, or heaven forbid (!) a day for yourself is a manufactured weapon of patriarchy. No offence, men, I don't hear guilt from them. And they have five hours more leisure time a week than we do.

I want you to think seriously about the idea that you don't have time for this. Really, really ponder it. Take into account everything else you've learned – about yourself, society and clothes – in this book alone.

Feminist author Caitlin Moran has pointed out that if you're in an equal partnership, you would assume 50 per cent of the workload. If you, as the woman/wife/mother are doing 70 per cent of the workload… that means you're picking up 20 per cent of someone else's work.

Yes, the work needs to be done. But does it need to be done by *you*?

What else could you do with that time? Might I suggest a dress-up session that will increase your style confidence, add more outfits to your roster, and save you lots of time in the long-term?

But playing dress up is...

Childish? Silly? A waste of time? Or a necessary creative exercise?

If we know that clothing informs identity, how fun to try on various personas! To imagine what your life could look like if you lived as *this* woman permanently! I can guarantee there are outfits in your wardrobe you've never considered – and it's not because you lack creativity. It's because you've never taken the time to find them.

But do you see yourself as a creative person? And does it matter?

I had a client, let's call her Natasha, who worked in tech. Natasha felt quite invisible but she had big plans for a promotion. Thanks to good-girl conditioning, just like Natasha, we believe that if we work really, really, really hard and don't rock the boat, one day our boss will finally see our potential and give us a pay rise based on merit. But sorry sweetie, that just ain't the way business goes.

You have to learn to manage up, and manage down, and look like the next leader of the company whilst you're doing it.

Why is wardrobe so fundamental?

One study showed that leaders with style are seen as more competent. Conversely, those who are seen as dated are assumed to have dated skills, too. Whilst Natasha was great at her job... *she wasn't getting the promotion.* Her skillset said, 'Way too good for this place, give her a pay rise' but her wardrobe said, 'Don't look at me.'

Her lack of confidence in what to wear also meant she wasn't doing career-building work like defining her personal brand, posting on LinkedIn, or networking regularly.

Twice in my career I got a pay rise because I was headhunted for other jobs. I twigged pretty early that the job I had at the time was not my career, and no one else was responsible for managing this but me. If I wanted to go from the measly £11,000 pa junior reporter salary (yes really) to an editor who increased her salary with speaking gigs, consulting and lecturing on the side, people had to know who I was, and I couldn't afford humility about my achievements.

Despite your boss knowing you're an asset, they won't hand out money willy-nilly. And if you get a bad boss, they'll probably take credit for your work. Make yourself indispensable, then make yourself a brilliant brand ambassador by looking the part and being well-known.

Natasha started off by telling me that this was simply a means to an end, she completely understood why her wardrobe was the missing piece but she had not a creative bone in her body. 'I'm analytical,' she said, 'I'm all about systems, I can't be creative.'

I challenged this on two grounds. Firstly, you can systemise style if that's the way that works for you. Secondly, the word "can't" is a problem. Remember: your brain will never make you a liar, so it will delete, distort, and generalise based on your belief.[4]

In Natasha's life, there was plenty of evidence of creativity. The

---

4. Young, E. (2018b) *Lifting the lid on the unconscious.* https://www.newscientist.com/article/mg23931880-400-lifting-the-lid-on-the-unconscious/.

new system she'd created to reduce waste, the quick-thinking solution that saved her boss a headache, the dance class she went to weekly. Creativity wasn't the problem – it was the *belief* she wasn't creative that had her overlooking the truth.

From a young age, Natasha had been told to pick the sensible options. And by sensible, people meant masculine. Things seen as stable, productive… and boring as hell!

Natasha chose the path set out for her: go to school, get good grades, go to college, get a job, work hard, retire…

The story was "creativity = no money."

How many times have you heard about the starving artist? It's not simply that we're told no one pays for art (lies, hello Taylor Swift/Beyoncé) – it's the trope that creative people are somehow irresponsible, flaky, and don't have their shit together. Creativity is equated to hippy-dippy, naked-in-the-woods, what-day-is-it, living-in-a-tent vibes.

Creativity is not rewarded in our system. You are given a gold star for repeating what the teacher just said to you. There is very little room for analytical thinking and even when you think a little differently, the teacher reads your answer next to a framework, decided by some exam board and of course, through their own lens of the world.

I remember receiving a terrible mark on an essay because my interpretation of the book was not "the correct answer." But that's the thing with creativity; why is there a correct answer? Without the freedom of creativity, we wouldn't have the finest works of art or music.

And to zoom in on our daily lives, we would not have the laptop on which I am currently writing this book, or the printing press which printed this book and allowed you to hold it in your hands. We would not have the technology which, I am assuming, brought your awareness to this book.

Everything person-made in the world around you began as an idea. Your coffee cup. The music you're listening to. The headphones through which you're listening. It is all a product of imagination. And inside imagination, there is no right or wrong.

Chapter 16

Let's Get in the Wardrobe (Finally)

Your wardrobe audit is not a tidy-up. It's a ritual of deciding who you're done being and who you're becoming.

Keep, toss, donate: likely that's a way you've sorted your wardrobe before. But why are you back to square 1 in a matter of months, doing "keep, toss, donate" all over again? It's because this system is surface-level, based only on practicalities and not on what your wardrobe *actually* is – the physical manifestation of your beliefs.

If you're not asking the right questions about how items came to be in your wardrobe, you won't learn anything from them.

I know you have a propensity for guilt, you love wearing that shit like a cape over every outfit. So the idea of getting rid of items, especially ones you may not have worn, makes you want to run and hide in the wardrobe (not that there's currently room). What if you viewed each item instead as a lesson, meaning there is no money wasted?

Cleansing your wardrobe in this new way is not simply a matter of cleansing items from your wardrobe. It's also about cleansing your mindset of old beliefs and stories. As long as those old beliefs and stories are running the show, you'll keep clearing out your wardrobe and wondering why you still have nothing to wear. You'll keep buying things under the guise that they will somehow transform you, but not wearing them and getting bored of them in a few weeks.

I don't believe those traditional wardrobe clean outs work. Without addressing the behaviour and working on the inner beliefs which inform that behaviour, things will go back to normal in your wardrobe (and in your life) faster than you can say BNWT.

The process (is yours)

There isn't a compulsory way to sort your clothes. The process is yours, so adapt it as you wish. I hate the thought of you getting so caught up in "but the book said to do it exactly like *this*" that it paralyses you.

You'll notice that there's plenty of blank space. I don't mean literally – what kind of crappy book would that be? I mean in terms of how this process goes. I'm giving you the outline. But ultimately, as this book is more about self-permission than it is about clothes, the real gift is the opportunity to make it your own.

I understand that right now it might feel like that moment you learn to ride a bike without stabilisers: you look behind you and realise your dad is way back in the distance and although you're doing it! You're riding the damn bike unaided! you think 'holy fuck!' and crash into a tree.

It feels that way because you're so used to being told what to do. But let me ask you this – *if being told what to do works so well, why are you here?*

Likely you've read the other style books. You follow all the style influencers. You might have even worked with a personal stylist.

Being told what to do might be what you want – but it's not what you *need*.

Clients sometimes find it frustrating at the start of the process when they ask me, 'Does this look OK?' and – provided of course we've covered some of the basics of styling – my response is 'What do you mean by OK? And why is it important for me to tell you it's OK?'

'I don't know, I don't know,' they say – but you *do*.

The answers to 'What should I wear?' are not in this book. They're not on social media. They're not held inside anyone else's opinions, on a podcast, or in whatever your partner/friend/sister thinks. The answers are within you.

It's time to put yourself back in control. You've set the destination and now you're the one who has to get into the driving seat.

It's a work event you can't get out of

This is how to approach this process: it's compulsory. If it's in your diary, it's as good as cast in stone. Immovable, solid, not to be fucked with. Go into your calendar right now and pick a date to make this happen. For added accountability, sign up at www.justgetdressed.com and I'll check in with you.

Yes, I know, you've got priorities. We covered this before, baby. It cost me extra dollars in ink to state it very clearly in BIG WORDS on previous pages. Don't make me write it out again. My editor will not be impressed at the repetition and I will get disgruntled Amazon reviews.

This is an event you can not get out of. I would say "like your wedding day" but even that's more cancellable than this. If he's a loser, don't marry him. Instead, do this wardrobe-shifting, identity-activating work, level the hell up in what you believe you're worthy of, and go get better.

Set your state

We're only doing this when we feel good. This is the one *absolute* rule. If you are someone who has periods and hormones that send your body 14lbs north of where it was five minutes ago on certain days of the month, and this is one of those days, avoid this exercise for now. We're done with the "I hate myself" spiral. Trying on clothes when you already feel on the brink of tears is not a good idea. I wouldn't do it, even though my wardrobe is one of my favourite spaces.

When you *are* feeling good and you're ready to do this, take some deep, belly-filling breaths. As you exhale, imagine you are pushing away any negative energy, clearing yourself of any old stories, patterns, and beliefs. As you inhale, imagine you are inviting in new, positive thoughts, and ask to feel excited about the outfits you might uncover today.

You can also do this with fragrance, a favourite show – whatever gets you in that "I can boss this" state of mind. Setting your state is a powerful tool not just for this moment, but for life. And once you've optimised your wardrobe, clothing can be one of the tools you use.

You might have heard the term "anchoring" which is essentially what we're talking about here. You can elicit a specific emotional state by using a physical item or sensory trigger that you associate with that state. For example, lots of my clients find it beneficial to set their state for work, especially if they work from home. You can use accessories, like earrings or shoes, to indicate to your brain that it needs to switch from rest mode to work mode.

You'll want to set aside a few hours for your wardrobe sort. This exercise can be physically and emotionally draining. Physically because you'll be lifting, folding, cleaning. Emotionally because the categories we use in this process are much deeper than "do I like this in this moment right now?"

A word on rash decisions

There is power in the decision to change. What we're really cleaning up when we clear out your wardrobe is your energy. However, impulsivity is likely what got your wardrobe into this mess… so why would impulsivity be the thing you need to sort it out?

If you are genuinely torn over an item… *leave it.*

Please don't get so caught up in your conditioning to follow the rules that you're under pressure to get rid of things just because The Style Editor put it in her process. You know yourself much better than I know you (and you'll know yourself on another level by the end of this process).

Place the things you're struggling with aside and we can come back to them another day. Mull them over. Sleep on your decision. It might be not that you don't know, but that you don't *know* you know (try saying that after an espresso martini). The answer has yet to surface.

When I am working long term with a client, we don't do one wardrobe day and that's it, finito, see ya. I'll come back a few months down the line because as their confidence grows, the things required from their wardrobes change. I'll often find they have no problem saying goodbye to items with which they previously struggled, because they've changed their belief about their identity and that item no longer aligns.

Recently a client was struggling with a bag. She asked me how she could tell if she'd elevated past it, or if she was just a bit bored.

'If you think about who you'll be this time next year, does that version of you have this bag?' I asked. The answer was no. Therefore, she knew it was time to let go.

Ask yourself the same question about items you're struggling with, and be as honest as possible. 'If I think about myself a year from now, would I wear this?'

No: time to let go. Yes: hold on, but you must wear it *now*. The magic of clothes does not work if you do not wear them.

Another exercise you can use to decide on the undecided is the hanger trick. Start with all your hangers facing the same direction. When you wear an item, turn the hanger around. After three months, assess how many items you haven't worn.

The initial assessment

Before we touch anything, open your wardrobe and answer the following questions:

- What is my immediate reaction or feeling about what I see?
- Is the way I store my items conducive to dressing well?
- How long does it take me to find new or exciting outfits?
- How often am I defaulting to the same things because it feels stressful or overwhelming?

- Do I immediately see any gaps in my inventory? Is there an abundance of one type of item, and a dearth of another?
- If this were a stranger's wardrobe, what would I assume about who they are as a person?
- Do I need any additional storage solutions?
- Does this look like the wardrobe of the woman who I want to be?
- If I could wave a magic wand and change this wardrobe, what would it look like?

Vision board your dream 'drobe

We've created a vision for our ideal style, life goals, and money-making plans. Now let's make one specifically for what you want your wardrobe to look like. Whilst you may not have the space to create the things you see on Pinterest (yet), there will likely be some ideas you *can* use. Maybe you like the way jewellery is stored, or shoes are stacked. You can use these as a frame of reference for what you want your end result to look like. Spending a little time considering whether your current space works, and implementing even the smallest of changes, can have a profound effect on your personal style.

Your environment shapes your self-perception as well as your behaviour. Our brains are wired to respond to stimuli, by-passing conscious decision-making on certain cues. The basal ganglia (a cluster of neurons in your brain) are associated with habit formation, conditional learning, procedural movement, motor control, and emotion.[1] They link what we do with what

---

1. Rocha, G.S. *et al.* (2023) 'Basal ganglia for beginners: the basic concepts you need to know and their role in movement control,' *Frontiers in Systems Neuroscience*, 17, p. 1242929. https://doi.org/10.3389/fnsys.2023.1242929.

we see. That's why you don't have to think about brushing your teeth. It's how you arrive at your destination with very little recollection of the drive.

Shifting around your wardrobe challenges your brain and forces you to address habitual behaviours that could be detrimental to your style.

Get it on the rail

Whilst acknowledging the privilege of having the space to do this: I find it helpful to use a self-assembly clothes rail for this process. You can use the rail to keep things organised, then later for creating outfits. It may also come in handy as we get into the stage of weekly outfit planning.

You can buy rails relatively cheaply online, though it's worth investing in one with durability – you will quickly discover, when you begin lifting items out of your wardrobe, how heavy they can be.

Take it all out

Now is not the time for being half-arsed. Get your full arse in the game and take all your clothes out. Feeling the physical weight of these items, if it's safe and practical for you to do so, will put everything into perspective.

And most importantly, how are you creating the life of your dreams with dead spiders and moths tucked away in the back of your wardrobe?

Get everything out and spend some time giving every shelf, rail, and piece of (floor)drobe a good clean. Now take stock. How does looking at everything in the light of day make you feel? Perhaps you are excited at the possibility of new outfits you're about to find. Maybe you've uncovered things you love, but had forgotten. Maybe you're already seeing things that need to go, if you're going to dress to your vision.

Or perhaps it's overwhelming. Perhaps you are seeing patterns, the results of the beliefs and habits that have been running your wardrobe over the years.

Sort into these categories:

- Clothes you love and wear
- Clothes you love and don't wear
- Clothes you don't love, but wear
- Clothes you don't love and don't wear

The first thing we do is remove clothes you **don't love and don't wear.**

'But Samantha, if I get rid of all the clothes I don't love or wear I'll have nothing left!'

If your wardrobe is full of things you don't wear, why are you holding onto them? What are you *really* holding onto?

Time and again I see this with my clients, and it may be true for you: it's less about the top or coat itself, and more about not quite having to become who we said we would become. Clothes we hate act as an anchor, weighing us down in our current reality, which does not reflect our most secret and biggest dreams.

The version of you that we mapped out earlier can stay as a figment of your imagination so long as you don't have to dress like her. When you're wearing clothes you don't like, you affirm your identity as not simply a current version of yourself, but a version of yourself from the past.

But it's a waste of money if I get rid of these things, you think as you pull barely-worn clothing from your wardrobe.

This is the sunk cost fallacy: our tendency to continue with something we feel we've invested heavily in, even when that thing is breaking us. Even when the smarter move would be to quit. Knowing when to walk away from something that's not working, or not helping you towards your biggest goals, or simply does not bring you joy, is a skill a winner must master. Not quitting isn't noble. It just means you'll end up being mediocre at lots of things (and feeling like a crappy person in the process) – and not genius at something specific.

In your wardrobe, this weird obsession with not being a quitter manifests as holding onto a totally impractical item from 10 years ago that you can't even get one arm into. Refusing to change your mind or let go is not only stubborn, it has dangerous implications in contexts outside your wardrobe. As new information comes to light, you may need to reflect on, or think critically about, a decision you're making. For example, you've committed to buying a particular house, you've got the survey done, you've planned the renovations, but then the flood report comes in and it's not good. Rather than change your mind, you stick with your original decision because you've already put so much time and effort and money into it — despite the fact that it will definitely cost you many, many times more in the future (in cash and emotional energy) when it floods.

That said, if you want to be a winner you must learn to focus on sustained effort towards something specific, and be ruthless about everything that sidetracks you from the goal. This is very hard to do for those who identify as female in a digital world, when so many distractions and expectations compete for our time and attention. Those distractions include anything in your wardrobe that you don't love, and don't wear. And that is why it's so important to remove them.

Bad energy and wardrobe woo

If the items you don't want to get rid of aren't about holding onto value in the economic sense, then what are you really holding onto?

Energy.

Many of my clients are surprised to find that in the days and weeks after going through the wardrobe cleansing process, they make more money. Opportunities seem to appear from nowhere. Metaphorical and physical doors open. In part, this is because their self-perception has shifted. They now see themselves as someone who stands by their word, takes action, and (finally!) starts wearing the clothes they love, instead of making do with the same five crappy items that feel meh.

But it's *also* because we've literally shifted energy-blocking shit from their wardrobes.

> "Everything is energy and that's all there is to it. Match the frequency of the reality you want and you can not help but get that reality. It can be no other way. This is not philosophy. This is physics."

Not the words of some influencer you'd roll your eyes at; these are words often incorrectly attributed to Einstein, but more they're likely a summary of his work.

Imagine if school taught physics using real-life examples, such as how our clothing could impact what we bring into our lives. I'd have definitely paid more attention in class, and maybe wouldn't have accidentally set my hair on fire (a story for another day).

How we define our reality is how we *experience* our reality. Everything is operating at a vibrational frequency (you, me, and yes, your clothes). Known as cymatics, scientists have discovered that sound waves create shapes. The study of vibrational frequency in this way is thought to trace back over 1,000 years to African tribes.[2] In the 1960s, Swiss scientist Hans Jenny conducted a series of experiments that showed how different waves created different patterns in sand. Low frequencies made basic patterns, high frequencies made more complex patterns.[3] Jenny believed that unlocking the mystery of waves and vibrations opened the door to the power of the universe.

If everything has a frequency, doesn't it make sense that clothing in higher frequencies will elevate *your* frequency? Linen has long been revered for its health properties and, like wool, it has a frequency of 5,000 hertz (Hz). This is 50 times the natural frequency of the human body. By contrast polyester, which is a synthetic, petroleum-derived material, has a frequency often measured below 100 hertz.[4]

Clothes you **don't love but wear** suffocate your potential and kill your vibe.

---

2. cymascope.com

3. Johnson, A. (2018) *Hans Jenny and the Sound Matrix – Shockwave-Sound blog and articles.* https://www.shockwave-sound.com/blog/hans-jenny-and-the-sound-matrix/.

4. A 2003 study by Dr Heidi Yellen widely referenced online. The results have not been validated by the scientific community. Yellen, H. *et al.* (2012) *Life-Giving Linen.* https://soundhealingresearchfoundation.org/wp-content/uploads/2024/08/Frequency-of-Fabric.pdf.

You may understand the concept of Cost Per Wear (the theory that you divide the cost of an item of clothing by number of wears to ascertain its value), but now consider Emotional Cost by Wear (or Not Wear). If you were to assign a monetary value to each item of clothing based on how it makes you feel, how often you wear it, and the stories attached, you would likely find the emotional cost of keeping it far outweighs what you originally paid.

Most people dress with little intention. Putting on your outfit is a small daily action that over a year makes a huge difference; it's the dressing compound effect.

The dressing compound effect

Day one, you have nothing to wear because your wardrobe is in a proper state, so you throw on that same pair of leggings and T-shirt and head for your coffee machine, before setting up at your desk. With a yawn, you open your calendar and see you'd pencilled in to record some social media content. Face-to-camera is important in your line of work. Potential clients take a long time to warm up and how are they going to believe you're the person for them if they never see you?

But… *not today.* You're not dressed for it. So you fill your day with less meaningful tasks, things with which a CEO would not really be concerning themselves. Tomorrow you'll make the videos. Except when tomorrow comes, your wardrobe is still a mess, you still have nothing to wear, so not today, maybe tomorrow…

Over and over this pattern repeats, until it's months later and the things you said you would do are hanging around your to-do list like a bad smell.

You can see where I'm going with this, right?

And I can see where you're going: *nowhere.*

Do you want December 31 to roll around and your progress to be minimal? Do you want to be filled with regret at all the things you didn't do and the progress you didn't make? Or do you want to be full of pride, thinking, *Yes queen, you really went for it this year?*

One of these options begins with unintentional daily dressing. The other begins with *intention.*

Think of yourself as a pilot, and every outfit as a chance to course-correct. The 1-in-60 Rule refers to the aviation rule of thumb and it's one of my favourite examples to demonstrate the importance of intention. For every 60 units of distance (e.g., nm, km, miles), a 1-degree heading error translates to 1 unit of distance off track.

That means if you don't correct an error early on, you'll end up way off where you wanted to go.

Clothes you love but don't wear

The not wearing generally comes down to one of two things:

1. Practicalities
2. Mindset

The formula for a functioning wardrobe = you can wear anything in it today with no excuses.

(Exception: extreme weather, which I admit is becoming more of a concern, thanks to climate change, a problem to which our overconsumption of clothes is contributing.)

If you have an excuse for not wearing specific items, then the item has a problem.

We'll tackle **practical first.**

You get a dopamine hit from bagging that satin bias-cut dress that feels so delicate and whimsical, it could be mistaken for a handkerchief. You convince yourself it would be great for a yacht party. But the reality is you live hundreds of miles from the ocean, you get sea sick and your muddy dog's paws do not mix with delicate satin.

For us to reap the benefits of enclothed cognition, we have to wear the items we associate with the next-level self.

Practical issues mean the item isn't working. Rather than procrastinating on making a decision (which, BTW, is still making a decision) – it's time to let it go.

Now, **mindset**.

There's no physical barrier to wearing these items, but emotionally you're uncomfortable. Whether it feels "too much", you're worried about ruining it, you don't feel confident enough to pull it off, or you're worried about the way you think you look in the item, use the tools in this book to get to the root belief and tackle it. Then, you have two options.

One – integrate.

I should have put an exclamation mark as if whisking up a spell – *integrate! And voilà – you shall go to the ball!*

If only it were that simple. But like I said before, I ain't no fairy godmother. Integration requires (yes, you guessed it) a little more work. One of my favourite exercises for integration is to *act as if.*

Just Get Dressed

Remember way back in the first part of this process where we mapped out your vision? What does that woman's day look like? Is she hurriedly grabbing a weak-as-piss coffee from a that-will-do machine at the petrol station on the way to a meeting she'll definitely be late for? Or does her day feel more leisurely than this?

Is she running around here, there and everywhere? Or is she, instead, going to work at that gorgeous hotel down the road? The one you're currently telling yourself you never have the time or the money to go?

Here's the thing about your lack of time and money: lack of time and money begets lack of time and money. In order to *become* you have to *be*. Your challenge is to put that item on and go sit in that fancy hotel. A cup of tea or coffee will set you back around the same amount as at your local coffee chain, where the tables are always dirty, the Wifi is dodgy, and the coffee beans are burned.

Discovering this little trick was a revelation in my own life. As soon as I stopped cheaping out on myself, other people stopped cheaping out on me. Much like with the frequency of the fabrics you wear raising your vibe, spending time in spaces that are high vibe raises your energy and acts like a magical invisible barrier to bullshit.

Not too long ago, I was meeting someone in a city centre, but their train was delayed. I had about an hour to kill and because every moment is spent right now on my book, I thought, *Great, I'll go to a coffee shop, whip out my laptop, and get some words on the page.*

I walked right up to the door of the generic coffee shop where there's always a child screaming and crumbs on the tables, placed my hand on the door… and stopped. If I want this book to have the impact it should, every word needs to be written with intention. If I am going to help my clients make true change in their wardrobes, make more money, and have more agency, I have to practise what I preach. I knew that stepping inside that noisy, busy coffee shop was like stepping back to a previous version of myself. Where I really needed to go was forward.

So I walked five minutes up the road to a historic hotel with a famous bar. I was serene. Quiet, clean, plush. Everything said luxury. I even spotted a celeb or two. I bought myself a coffee – for no more than it would have cost at the coffee chain – and managed to get some work done. And it wasn't a simple case of hashing out some words; I really felt like the energy of what I'd written was so much more potent than it would have been.

Since then, I've made a point of setting up my environment in a way that feels beneficial to my book-writing and as a result, I'm taking better actions to support it. I'm creating content about book-writing, I'm putting the feelers out for speaking opportunities. I'm organising a launch event.

The me who stays in "that will do, chain coffee shop" energy is the me who talks herself out of celebrating the fact she wrote a book by having a launch party. The me who stays in "that will do, chain coffee shop" energy is the me who doesn't ask to be on that podcast or speak at that event. That me would procrastinate on all the important stuff, whilst placating her ego with inconsequential busy work.

The other option for **clothes you love but don't wear is**: remove them from your wardrobe.

And if that suggestion makes you want to scream into your sequins, you know what that's telling you. It's telling you to go back to option one. Spoiler: that really is the only option. It's the only option because when things we love hang unworn in our wardrobes, they have no benefit. In fact, they have a negative impact. Each time you open the doors of your closet and see them, you're reminded of all the things you're not. You aren't wearing those things you love the idea of, because you aren't taking the actions you want to take.

One of my clients bought a beautiful dress in early summer. On a rainy, grey September day, we had a session and under her desk, still in its beautiful packaging, she discovered that dress. There had been plenty of occasions during the long, hot, hazy summer to wear such an item, but she hadn't. Not due to impracticality, but identity.

Clothes you love and wear

Whenever I begin working with a new client, I ask them to tell me about their wardrobe. Generally their answers are overwhelmingly negative.

This isn't working. I hate that. I can never find anything. I don't know how to.

And because their wardrobes are symbolic for other areas of their lives, we notice patterns emerging between their clothing struggles and their business ones. Maybe they have lots of clothes they don't wear because they're lacking the confidence to be that woman, and that lack of confidence bleeds into their job where they're too scared to ask for a pay rise. Maybe they feel clueless about putting outfits together because they're unsure what they want their style to say and this bleeds over into their relationship where they hold off sharing their feelings effectively with their partner.

Studies show humans tend to have negativity bias: "the propensity to attend to, learn from, and use negative information far more than positive information."[5] So when asked a neutral question like, "Tell me about your wardrobe" we're more likely to list all the things we don't like than the things we do.

You could make the salient point that no one who feels totally happy about their style is going to seek the help of a personal stylist. And whilst that is correct, generally I find the clients who make the most money are the ones who come at this work with optimism.

We've done a lot of stuff on beliefs by this point, so you know how this goes – you're deleting, distorting, and generalising based on what you've convinced yourself is correct.

If you work with a personal stylist and your attitude is that none of this matters and all my clothes are crap, you won't be open to suggestions. That poor personal stylist can try their best, be as enthusiastic as a clown at a five-year-old's birthday party, and it won't matter – you've already decided nothing here works.

This book is here to help you understand why you have nothing to wear, what to do about it, and help you to rediscover (or perhaps discover for the first time) the joy to be found in your clothes.

Joy in getting dressed is a rebellion in a capitalist culture that functions on the basis you'll keep believing it's not for someone like you.

---

5. Vaish, A., Grossmann, T. and Woodward, A. (2008) 'Not all emotions are created equal: The negativity bias in social-emotional development.,' *Psychological Bulletin*, 134(3), pp. 383–403. https://doi.org/10.1037/0033-2909.134.3.383.

Finding the joy means looking for the positives in your wardrobe as well as removing things that don't work. When you look through the lens of optimism, you'll likely find there is some good stuff here. You, my friend, have the potential for great style. And the easiest route for getting there? By looking for the things you already like. Clothes you love and wear give us a sense of direction. They're the thing we're inputting into the satnav. What do you enjoy about these specific items? Is it how they make you feel? Is it the ease with which you can wear them?

Be careful not to confuse "love and wear" with "functional."

This is where having a benchmark figure comes in. How good do you need to feel every day to get the minimum things done that would move you forward in life and business? I am a service provider, so it's important that my potential clients get to know me. You've likely come across me in some capacity before picking up this book, because I've been visible. I've consistently been talking to you, through written word, through video and podcast, for years. The minimum I need to do in my business each day is show up in some capacity. And to do that, I need to feel good.

If I were to put a numerical figure, one being "troll under a bridge" and 10 being "Mariah Carey after they defrost her on December 1" where do I need to be on the scale of Diva in order to show up and give it your all? I've decided it's an eight. Therefore, everything in my wardrobe and the outfit combinations I create must feel like an eight.

Whilst some level of functionality is always required in our clothes (if you can't sit down and feel comfortable, what the fuck is the point?) that never wins out over my other requirements.

What to do next

Hang the clothes you love and wear, and the clothes you love and *are working on wearing,* on your rail. Now take a moment to re-assess.

- What patterns do you notice? Are there repeating shapes, colours, textures, or styles?
- Do you have lots of items in one category and hardly any in another?
- What would prevent you from creating wearable outfits with these items?
- Have you spotted any new outfits amongst these clothes?
- Where are the glaringly-obvious gaps? Does this inventory feel like it could comfortably take you through the next season – of weather and of your life?
- Take photos of each individual item.

As we covered during the vision-building phase, you are more likely to wear what you can see. Keeping a running inventory of all your clothing in your head is unrealistic. Document your wardrobe digitally and you will save yourself time, money, and stress. There are apps you can use to build a virtual version of your closet.

Get in your pants, it's time for a massive try-on session

You may have categorised some items as keepers that, on reflection, you decide to ditch. With each item, remember you're assessing against your vision and your benchmark.

Make a separate pile of anything that needs alteration, cleaning or repair – then take out your calendar and book in the time to get it done. If you do not do this, you may as well not bother. Those clothes will stay in a bag by the front door for the next six months, causing nothing but agitation.

Have a go at creating outfits. Go unhinged! Off the wall! Don't let "that wouldn't go together" stop you. Actually *give it a try*. Your assumptions are getting in the way of serious outfit potential. It's mix-and-match season, baby.

Take photos of every outfit that passes your vibe check. Either keep these in a gallery on your phone, or in a digital wardrobe app. For the super-organised amongst us, you might like adding the images to your calendar, so that you know what you're wearing, when.

This takes away decision fatigue, saves you so much time, helps you feel excited about what you get to wear this coming week, and gets you walking in the literal shoes of the woman you want to be.

Chapter 17

No One Dies, It's Just Clothes

Experimentation without self-judgement.

Every time I go through my wardrobe, I have a renewed sense of appreciation for my wardrobe, and more confidence in styling myself.

As much as this book will help you understand clothes are not just clothes, they also… *are.*

Whilst you might be astounded at the bigness of some of the concepts inside this book, and that you are wearing beliefs and patterns put in motion long before you were born, I would invite you to remember that the opposite is *also* true.

No one dies, it's just clothes.

The entire point of uncovering the bigness is so that we get to come back here to this – clothes don't matter just as much as they do.

You likely don't need to spend a dime to create new looks for yourself. What you need is (yep, you guessed it) self-trust. And the ability to suspend self-critique whilst you try. You attempt a pair of jeans and they don't fit? Means nothing about you as a person. You try an outfit combination and it doesn't work? So what! What does something "working" really mean, anyway?

Does it simply mean "to fit"? Are you going to define yourself by such a low standard as "I can get into this"?

Outfits are a case of personal preference. Someone else could look at what you created and think it was a work of art. And even if the outfit isn't hitting, it's never wasted – you're learning, growing, and getting out of your comfort zone.

We've spent a great deal of this book uncovering the hidden meaning of your clothes, and perhaps now you think *Samantha, you absolute hypocrite* as I urge you to let go of meaning.

Suspend, just for the sake of experimentation in this try-on phase, any notion about what you can't wear or what does or doesn't go together.

Task 1: An unlikely pairing

From your wardrobe, select two pieces you would never dream of wearing together. Why would you not wear these together? Is it because they don't go? And what does "go together" really mean? How much are the rules you've been taught to follow impacting the amount of liberation you have to experiment?

Even the experiments you've done in the past are based on rigid rules. Remember in chemistry class, when you were tasked with making different interactions (and perhaps you too were wearing a dick-covered lab coat)? To experiment is "the action or process of trying out new ideas, methods, or activities." But in the education system, this means new to *you* – not new entirely.

Yes, what you were doing with the Bunsen burner and the nitric acid was an experiment, but there was still a checklist printed out by the science teacher, and grades for best and worst performance.

There was a right and wrong way for this to go; you were supposed to put this liquid into the dish first, then add three jobs of that liquid using the pipette, making this more of a recipe than an experiment.

Does the outfit feel too much? Are you worried about feeling or looking ridiculous? And what does "ridiculous" mean? For one of my clients, her absolute no-no outfit was a denim shirt and jeans. She declared at the beginning of our try-on session that double-denim is something she wouldn't be seen dead in. So I asked her to try it.

Not only did she discover it was nowhere near as bad as she believed, everything we tried afterwards felt easy. She was less resistant to things she'd never tried because I'd already made her styling worst-nightmare come true and guess what – she was still here to tell the tale.

Task 2: Ask someone to style you

Good friends see our potential, not our flaws. You are looking at yourself through the lens of all your baggage. Your friends are looking at you through the lens of all your qualities. Choose someone you trust (and whose opinions on style, business, and life you value) and share with them your digital wardrobe, or ask them to come and take a look in your closet. Ask them what they see that you don't. Get them to put an outfit together for you, and then take them out for a drink somewhere fancy where you can live your best lives, to wear it.

At the end of your try-on, ask the following questions:

- How many new outfits have I discovered?
- What is my definition of an outfit that works?

- Where are old stories and beliefs still playing out in the way I dress?
- How far was I willing to go with my experimentation?
- How could I push the needle just a little more with what I try?

In your experimentation, you may have noticed some crucial items are missing from your inventory. If only you had a pair of knee-high boots, a good belt, or a waistcoat, you'd have more outfits.

Make a list of what you need and let's go shopping.

Part Seven

Get In Loser, We're Going Shopping!

Style has to evolve with us or sooner or later, we become sewn into a prison of our own making. The link between what we wear and how we feel is covered elsewhere in this book, and there are cases when shopping is unavoidable.

And – lean in close because I need to whisper this – shopping *can* be fun.

Style is self-expression and multiple truths can exist. It can be true that we must be mindful of our choices, do the inner work to avoid overconsumption, and be capable of a nuanced conversation regarding clothes. *And* it can also be true that sometimes, you do not have the fundamentals of a functioning wardrobe.

This book is not here to cast more shame, judgement or guilt upon you, or to make you feel bad about treating yourself. Fuck that, and fuck anyone who deems themselves so beyond reproach they can make others feel shame when when they make similar choices.

This is about shopping *with consideration*. It's about reviewing your existing wardrobe before you shop, examining your emotions, and getting to the root cause of why you want to shop, so that when you do it, you are as mindful as possible.

Chapter 18

Big Budgets and Behavioural Economics

The fashion industry has spent billions understanding your psychology so they can exploit it.

Fast fashion giants spend spectacular sums on psychologists, advertising, and marketing experts. They are always thinking about removing the obstacles between your credit card and their payment processor.

The area of research about what drives us to buy is called behavioural economics. According to *Psychology Today*: "[...] retailers may successfully manipulate the desire for a "good deal" by making an unneeded item seem especially affordable or portraying it as being in limited supply."[1]

Common strategies include classical conditioning: "training consumers to associate a product with certain cues through repeated exposure – creating a scarcity mindset (suggesting that a product only exists in limited quantities), or employing the *principle of social proof* to imply that everyone is buying a product – so you should, too."

Marketers may also employ heuristics, or mental shortcuts, to make a purchase seem like a no-brainer. One example of this is anchoring bias, which means your brain anchors into the first

____

1. *Consumer behavior* (2025). https://www.psychologytoday.com/us/basics/consumer-behavior.

piece of information it sees. As an example, you're told a dress is $500, but no sooner have you exited the shopping app than you're sent an email offering you 10 per cent off the dress, making the new price $450. Your brain anchored the first price – $500 – making the $50 discount seem substantial.

Then there's those little warnings that pop up in-browser that "100 people are looking at this right now!" Or "low in stock" or "this item is selling fast!" Tactics like this tap into loss aversion, a psychological phenomenon in which people are typically more worried about missing out on something than concerned about what they're gaining. The theory, developed by psychologists in the 1970s, says that the pain of losing something is almost twice as intense as the pleasure of gaining something of the same value.[2]

Free shipping removes friction at checkout, because even though we might be spending £200 we feel irked about that additional £4.99 fee. Shoppers are more likely to spend more to remove the shipping fee than swallow the shipping fee.

The market research industry is growing, and is reportedly worth over $54 billion.

In-store, retailers apply more psychological tactics, but with the majority of consumers saying they prefer in-person shopping, it's even more important they get it right. The entry point, or the decompression zone, is prime real estate. It sets the tone for your experience and understanding of the brand. Clutter and chaos gives the impression of low-prices; minimalism says luxury.

According to *Forbes*, the "racetrack layout" is a popular choice,

2. Kahneman, D. and Tversky, A. (1979) 'Prospect Theory: An Analysis of Decision under Risk,' *Econometrica*, 47(2), p. 263. https://doi.org/10.2307/1914185.

guiding shoppers on a path through the store.[3] Most shoppers instinctively turn right upon entering a store, so this is likely the area where you'll find the items they really want to sell.

Then there's "grouping" – where items that relate to each other are stocked together. Eye-line is also an important consideration, with premium items most likely to be right where you can see them. One study on the grocery industry found that more than 50 per cent of the products bought in the supermarkets were impulse purchases. Hence why you'll find offers at the ends of aisles.

Impulse zones are the areas you'll find near the tills: accessories, perfumes, or skincare are popular choices because they probably cost less than the total you're already paying and next to £200 of clothing, a £20 perfume doesn't feel like a big deal.

Heatmaps and customer tracking on camera highlight popular zones and dead ones. Lighting, music, and scent play important roles, too. When a piece of jewellery is sparkling under the lights and empowering music is playing, you're not buying the bracelet, you're buying the feeling. You're buying who you want to be; a promise of what you'll become with the necklace around your neck and your shoulders in the jacket.

Loyalty cards are another way of retaining customers. They tap into routine or habitual decision-making, because once a customer has a routine, they're less likely to go elsewhere.

---

3. Katz, E.Y. (2025) 'The Psychology of Retail: How Store Layout Impacts Sales,' *Forbes.* https://www.forbes.com/councils/forbesbusinesscouncil/2025/01/03/the-psychology-of-retail-how-store-layout-impacts-sales/

The shopping process

There are five factors in the shopping process: problem recognition (I need something new to solve a problem I'm having), information search (where can I find the thing I need?), evaluation of alternatives (this item, or that?), purchase decision (I'm going with this), and post-purchase behaviour.[4]

You may notice how each of the outlined tactics above hit a specific point in the buying cycle, but the area I'd like to focus on is problem recognition because for some purchases, like a lawnmower when you have an overgrown garden, there is a legitimate issue to fix. For others, like the compulsion to have a new dress when you have a wardrobe full of them, or to buy a new "miracle" cream to fix a "problem area" on your body, there is a concerted effort by manufacturers to make you see issues where previously there were none. For many thousands of years, humans have existed with body hair (in fact it was key to our survival), cellulite, blemishes, and wrinkles.

New forms of media squeeze the timeline between problem recognition and purchase decision. On Monday, you might be perfectly fine with your earlobes, but by Wednesday you are convinced they are too big/too small/too sticky-outy, and that to fix them you should buy a product you've seen everywhere – on your phone and laptop – many dozens of times in the space of 48 hours.

We are being tracked more than ever before; from the sites we visit online to the loyalty apps we use in-store, advertising is

---

4. Comegys, C., Hannula, M. and Väisänen, J. (2006) 'Longitudinal comparison of Finnish and US online shopping behaviour among university students: The five-stage buying decision process,' *Journal of Targeting Measurement and Analysis for Marketing*, 14(4), pp. 336–356. https://doi.org/10.1057/palgrave.jt.5740193.

getting more personalised, picking up clues about our mood, mindset, and habits. According to ex-Meta's Sarah Wynn-Williams, author of *Careless People*, the company actively targeted teenagers based on their emotional state.

"It could identify when they were feeling worthless or helpless or like a failure, and [Meta] would take that information and share it with advertisers," Wynn-Williams told US Senators.[5] Studies show you are more likely to shop through boredom, loneliness, or stress and that's why emotional regulation is vital when it comes to shopping.

The more aware you are of the tactics used not just to part you from your cash, but to get you into a part-with-your-cash mindset, the more in control of your style and finances you will be.

I'm really cautious of treating you like a fucking idiot and stating the obvious, but as someone who's been here multiple times, despite my intelligence and access to logic, I know it bears repeating. You're exposed to sales tactics way more times in a day than you realise, and it takes a hell of unthreading to detach yourself from the system we're all sewn up in.

The following steps are intended as reminders or pointers.

Recognise your buying triggers

Go back through your last 10 purchases and trace the journey from "not knowing I have a problem" to "it's delivered." What

---

5. *A time for Truth: Oversight of Meta's foreign relations and representations to the United States Congress | United States Senate Committee on the Judiciary* (2025). https://www.judiciary.senate.gov/committee-activity/hearings/a-time-for-truth-oversight-of-metas-foreign-relations-and-representations-to-the-united-states-congress.

started the buying cycle – a legitimate need, or an emotional trigger? Can you spot any patterns? For example, maybe you notice that each purchase happens in a low state, or as a reward for something.

Then examine your post-purchase behaviour. How long is it between the delivery of one product, and the "I have a problem" moment which resulted in the purchase of the next? Do you make good use of the things you buy, or do you barely get use from one product before buying another?

Tick it off the "when to shop" list

If a purchase is solving a legitimate problem, or fulfilling a legitimate need, it's not something to feel awful about. Go through the "when to shop" list and see if you have the green light or the red light. Remember, you can't fool yourself. If you know it's on the "when **not** to shop" list and you still do it anyway, there is something under the surface to address, and potentially with the support of a professional.

Implement a cooling-off period

Wanting something that popped up on your Instagram page at 11pm two wines deep on a shit day at the office is not the same as evaluating a purchase with a cool head in the cold light of day. Put it on your wishlist, sure, and if you still want it a few days from now and it fulfils a legitimate need, go ahead and buy it.

Checkout of the conversation, not the shopping cart

As soon as you hit that retailer's website, you're going to get a pop up offering you 10 per cent off in exchange for your email address. No big deal, you think. Worth it for the discount. Except now they're tracking you around the internet, learning your moods and behaviours and when to target you with new shiny things.

Sure it takes less than a second to swipe away an email when it pops up on your phone. But when you're doing that every day, multiple times a day, it adds up. You want to spend any of your precious life swiping away emails for the sake of saving £10 on a product you don't really need?

The cost of shopping isn't only on our own bank balances, peace of mind, and quality of life. We don't live in a bubble. Our shopping decisions have global consequences. So it's worth thinking about the process and our buying triggers in the wider context of the world we live in, too.

Chapter 19

Why We Need to Address Our Shopping Habits

The full human and environmental cost of fast fashion – and how we can break the cycle.

Scientists discovered a new mountain not too long ago in the Chilean desert. It's visible from space and growing by about 39,000 tonnes a year.

Rock? No. *Clothes.*

Meanwhile, on some beaches in West Africa you won't find white sand; you will find piles and piles of rags. Ghana has a huge used clothing market – most of it coming from the UK and USA. But this isn't a circular economy; it's reported that more than 100 million items go to waste each year in Accra, the capital of Ghana, alone.[1] This is often described as "waste colonialism" and when the Ghanaian government has attempted to reduce the deluge, taxes have been applied, or grant money withdrawn.[2]

According to campaigners for the Stop Waste Colonialism initiative:

---

1. James, L. (2022) 'Mountains of clothes washed up on Ghana beach show cost of fast fashion,' *The Independent*, 27 July. https://www.independent.co.uk/climate-change/news/fast-fashion-ghana-clothes-waste-b2132399.html.
2. stopwastecolonialism.org

"The ignorance of the Global North is aided by the fact that the language around clothing donation and recycling is often misleading. Respected charities claim that no garment donated to them will end up in a landfill. Municipal bins have recycling symbols on them and brand-managed take-back programs and clean-out kits claim to be part of a recycling program when much of the clothing that enters these programs will be sold on to the global secondhand market.

"From our perspective, waste colonialism is becoming more pronounced. The great acceleration of fast fashion in the 2000s has only intensified the Global North's reliance on Kantamanto [a textile market in Accra] as an outlet for excess clothing and in turn the lowering quality of fast fashion leaves Kantamanto retailers dependent on a system where they have to sell higher quantities of a cheaper product to stay out of debt, creating a vicious cycle."

A report in early 2024 said consumers living in high-income countries should limit themselves to five new items per year if we want to keep the planet's rise in temperature to target. I know you're probably thinking: 'But even if I reduce what I buy, retailers will still produce clothing.'

There will certainly be a lag time between us making new habits and retailers reducing their production, but wouldn't it be better to commit today, rather than say, 'Oh well, nothing I, just one woman, can do'?

But what CAN we do?

Whilst it's not my intention to shame, sometimes we need to have a harsh word to make very clear how pressing this matter is. "But what can you do!" said with a shrug, slaps of privilege. Yes, you are *one* woman. And imagine if every *one* woman reading this book wrote a letter to her government representative, or found petitions to sign, or researched initiatives to donate to, or even started their own initiatives and penned their own books.

It's imperative that we don't put it all on the women because fuck knows, and as we've explored within these pages, we have a lot of work on our plates already. But I hope the link between you feeling useless (a construct of a patriarchal society that's terrified of women's power) and the state of things far beyond your wardrobe is becoming clearer.

I hope "but what can I do?" becomes less of a rhetorical question, said with a shrug as you go back to sipping your Starbucks (a company that paid no corporation tax in the UK in 2025) and more of a rallying cry.[3] The most powerful word in the sentence is "I" because you have much more power than you could ever imagine.

As I'll keep asking you: who or what benefits when we shrug and turn away?

Your one action could be starting a conversation with your friends, daughters, sisters, or colleagues about the statistics on fast fashion and climate change within these pages.

---

3. Butler, S. (2025) 'Starbucks's UK retail business paid no corporation tax last year,' *The Guardian*, 15 April. https://www.theguardian.com/business/2025/apr/15/starbuckss-uk-retail-business-paid-no-corporation-tax-last-year.

Fast fashion giants are using sustainability as a buzzword to make you think you're making a better choice. Sustainable lines account for just one per cent of the fast fashion business, yet these new lines and initiatives have millions of dollars in advertising ploughed at them so we see those companies as the good guys or not all bad.[4]

And it isn't just the environment suffering long-term from our quickly-needed fashion fix. Often the uncomfortable answer to "who made my clothes?" is: Someone low-paid and badly treated.

For ALL women

In 2019, Oxfam found that zero per cent – *none* – of Bangladeshi garment workers earned a living wage. The fashion labour force is predominantly female.

This is a book for women about undoing centuries of conditioning that have led to us having nothing to wear. But for it to be a book that is *truly* for women, we can't ignore that women are the ones suffering at the hands of our overconsumption. Women-supporting-women spaces shouldn't mean supporting women but only those who look like us, have similar backgrounds to us, and can help us fund our businesses which are built under, and mimic, capitalistic patriarchy. We're strutting about in our new top knowing full well who made it… *and not giving a shit*.

Up to reading this section of the book, you could have pleaded ignorance. Now you can't.

---

4. Barber, A. (2021) *Consumed: The Need for Collective Change: Colonialism, Climate Change, and Consumerism*. Balance.

When you spend your money, you are making a vote for the kind of world in which you want to live. You think you have very little power to affect change. You do.

Some people argue that fast fashion production is vital to communities with low socio-economic growth because it provides employment. They also say that we shouldn't be blaming ourselves for the faults of a system because, well, don't women already have enough blame? I think that perspective seeks to absolve us of the part we play. I don't want feminism if it's white woman, certain-socio-economic-level, feminism. I want feminism for all.

Fashion contributor Bandana Tewari calls fast fashion "modern-day colonialism."[5] Says Liz Ricketts, an American fashion waste campaigner: "We have decided that convenience is a human right and we think that when we go shopping we should always be able to find exactly what we want. We should find it in our size and the colour that we want. That also contributes to this overproduction."[6]

If we stopped consuming so much, but were willing to pay more per item – and demanded that the money actually get into the hands of those who made our clothes – perhaps the world would be a little bit better. On a micro-level, we'd be forced to be more creative with our style because we'd have less stuff to choose from (and we'd also be less overwhelmed by it). On a macro-

---

5. Tewari, B. (2024) 'Op-ED │ How Fashion Perpetuates Modern-Day Colonialism,' *The Business of Fashion*, 25 September. https://www.businessoffash ion.com/opinions/global-markets/op-ed-how-fashion-perpetuates-modern-day-colonialism/.
6. Besser, L. (2021) *Dead white man's clothes: How fast fashion is turning parts of Ghana into toxic landfill.* https://www.abc.net.au/news/2021-08-12/fast-fashion-turning-parts-ghana-into-toxic-landfill/100358702.

level, we'd be raising the bar on what we're willing to allow in our names.

The chairman and former CEO of H&M Group is reportedly worth nearly $2 billion.[7] In Bangladesh, where around 600,000 people work for H&M, the average salary is $119 dollars.[8] H&M is one of the labels repeatedly found amongst those rag piles in Ghana. Yes, I'm aware the job of a CEO and that of a garment worker is different. No, I'm not saying let's burn the entire system to the ground and our bras along with it. I'm asking us to question our relationship with clothes because right now, we view them as a commodity, when they're anything but.

Our clothing production uses up finite planetary resources. One of the most polluted rivers in the world is the Buriganga, Bangladesh. It flows through the capital, Dhuka, serving as a water supply for millions.[9] Garment factories line the river and discharge toxic chemicals and heavy metals into the water. The cost of the outfit you bought isn't the true cost. Someone else is picking up the tab.

I'm not saying don't shop, or we shouldn't ever shop – or even that shopping isn't enjoyable. I'm saying our wardrobes are full of shit and we can do better. I promise, you don't have to have a trained eye to know if a garment is decent quality. In the main, the quality of what's available in the mainstream stores is declining rapidly. As brands speed up their production to match

7. https://www.goodreturns.in/karl-johan-persson-net-worth-and-biography-blnr2198.html

8. Adegeest, D.-A. (2024) 'Garment workers among the lowest-paid industrial workers globally,' *FashionUnited*, 5 January. https://fashionunited.uk/news/fashion/garment-workers-among-the-lowest-paid-industrial-workers-globally/2024010573416.

9. We Are Water Foundation (2018) *Where is our river?* https://www.wearewater.org/en/insights/where-is-our-river/

ultra-fast producers, they're shoving stuff in stores that, quite frankly, has no business being there.

You deserve better quality clothes

It's an unfortunate reality that a budget for clothing in a high street store will not get you anywhere near the same quality as a decade or even five years ago. Worldwide economic changes have increased costs, leading to corners being cut so brands can maintain their profits and, increasingly, our clothes are made from synthetic fabrics.

We think we're making the best financial decision by choosing 10 items for the same price as one. But it *shows*. The stuff doesn't hang as well, it doesn't fit as well, the material isn't as good and it doesn't last. Before you know it, you're buying replacements. Then more replacements. And isn't that exhausting? Don't you have better things to do with your time?

Recently, I visited a "comfort zone" store with a client. Synthetic satin blouses were shoved on rails, creased likely beyond repair. Bags were tossed on shelves literally covered in dust. Hangers screeched on metal rails in the sale section like fingernails down a chalkboard. It was overstuffed, hot, crowded, and noisy.

A moment later we walked directly across the road to the "out of reach" store and it was like drinking a cool glass of water on a hot summer's day. Everything was presented beautifully (there was even a member of staff steaming the shirts), it was tranquil and spacious, giving the buyer the time and (literal) space to think.

In a clustered environment where the mood is "everything must go NOW!" you are being encouraged to make hurried, irrational decisions. The chaos is disguising the things manufacturers don't want you to see – the broken zips, wonky stitching, uneven hems, and synthetic materials.

If budget genuinely is an issue, there are more ways than ever to find great clothes. The problem isn't a lack of decent quality pre-loved clothes. The problem is your lack of style strategy. Of course, going on eBay and searching for a generic term like "T-shirt" is going to leave you with millions of results, feeling overwhelmed, frustrated, and swearing off second-hand forever.

But going through the process outlined in this section will give you a better understanding of what you'd like your style to be, and that means you can narrow down your search and feel less overwhelmed.

Chapter 20

When to Shop

Now you know you're being manipulated, it's time to decide for yourself when to swipe your card – and when to walk away.

A style rut isn't a problem, it's an invitation. It only becomes a problem when you ignore the invitation. That's right, this is one party you can't decline with a "sorry, I'm washing my hair." You can stay home... but the party will find you there anyway.

It's like everything you're wearing is fine... but it's not *it*. And it goes beyond the mental or emotional – you can feel it in your body. It may manifest as sluggishness, or frustration. Perhaps you find yourself procrastinating, specifically on tasks that feel big and like they'll move your business forward. For example, maybe you want to write a book, but your ideas feel less like flow, more of a drip, and you can't seem to muster the motivation to put pen to paper (or hands to keyboard).

You find yourself scrolling through Instagram for inspiration, but you'd be better off getting changed.

Being able to tune into what's under the surface of a style rut will serve you for life. Since the universe is in a state of expansion, and since we are creatures of evolution, you could argue it's your life purpose to consistently grow.

You have an inventory problem

I'm not your fairy godmother. I can't wave a magic wand and turn pumpkin-level items into princéss-worthy outfits. In my experience, most women's wardrobes have a deluge of clothes, but often they are missing the practicals needed for cohesive looks. But sometimes, the wardrobe is missing items altogether, or what's in there is poor quality, or has not been maintained or updated in a long time, and therefore, does not make the wearer feel good.

The current state of your wardrobe matters. If your wardrobe consists of worn-out, ill-fitting, or low-quality pieces that don't align with your goals, I will advise parting ways with them. I can't create high-level positioning from a foundation that doesn't support it.

My goal is to help you maximise what you already own, but in many cases, a few key pieces will be necessary to complete your wardrobe. You'll need to have a budget in mind.

Your identity has shifted

Being a woman comes with a lifetime of identity changes. From puberty, to menstruation, to childbirth, to perimenopause, our bodies are in a constant state of flux. And whilst that is a magical, life-giving force, instead of celebration, you're taught your body is something to feel ashamed of.

In conjunction with the physical, you will meet many different versions of yourself through the journey of life. You will take on roles like Graduate, Boss, Bride, Mother, Founder, sometimes one after another, sometimes all at once. You will uncover new layers of yourself – I've had clients who've found out they're adopted, or that they are neurodivergent.

It's like you're a jigsaw, and you collect all the pieces to form a picture called Life. Some of them fit perfectly, others need to be replaced from time to time. And each time one is added, or replaced, the picture shifts slightly.

You're out of date

You're not milk; you don't expire. But some of your clothes might be giving a whiff of cheesiness.

As you'll discover when we dive into the who, what, wear of fashion hierarchy, dated style can lead to all sorts of silly assumptions about your skillset. Nonetheless, it's something to be aware of. If not from a personal brand perspective, simply for the way you feel when your outfit is a vibe.

When NOT to shop

You're a grown woman, you can do whatever the fuck you want. But you're here because you're self-aware enough to work on areas that need improvement, including your relationship with clothes.

So rather than me telling you what to do, I will spell out some of the most common patterns, loops, or situations I observe that keep us in unhealthy shopping habits.

You're panicking about an event

I know this advice doesn't help you in the moment but you're not *in* the moment. You're in *another* moment, reading this book.

Which means you have time to prepare in advance so you can prevent panic-shopping from happening again.

Thanks to our need for external validation, we often place enormous pressure on ourselves to look a certain way for big events, so we can show the world how fabulous our lives are. But when it comes to the everyday reality of our fabulous lives? We make do with scruffy old tracksuit bottoms, a T-shirt way past its prime, and feel terrified that we're going to accidentally turn our cameras on for the Monday morning Teams call, sitting there in a smelly robe the dog uses as a blanket.

It would be far more beneficial to focus your attention on the everyday. If you spent your money on what you wear the most, you'd lift your energy – and you wouldn't worry about wearing an older dress to a wedding.

I witness women doing the panic-buy rigmarole when it comes to professional events as well as personal ones. We dream of giving talks on stages. We understand how it raises our profiles and brings in clients or opportunities at work. But when the opportunity arises, we *FREAK OUT*. The first place our minds go is: *What the hell should I wear?* And we hop on the panic-buy rollercoaster. When we finally settle on an outfit, we walk up to that stage… and break out in a cold sweat.

Our minds are filled with negativity like: *Who the hell do you think you are? No one's listening. They think you look ridiculous. You're a fraud, there's no way you deserve to be up here on this stage.*

Why? Because we have not integrated our identity to match the outfit. We bought the clothes with the best of intentions and placed them in the back of the wardrobe where they stayed for two months. We hoped the items had magical powers, that alone they could transform us. Meanwhile we sat around in the same old tracksuit bottoms and ~~dog blanket~~ dressing gown.

If we'd worn the outfit before presentation day, then presentation day would feel like another day at the office.

We'd deliver our talk with more confidence, because we could forget what we are wearing and focus on the words.

Next time you worry about what to wear to an event, consider the Invisible Guest Theory: in social situations, people focus on their own insecurities, perceived inadequacies, and appearance. You are essentially an invisible guest in their world, and you in theirs, and aren't being judged by others as much as you're judging yourself.

You're having a bad day

Buying stuff gives us a dopamine hit – but that's a distant memory by the time the "thanks for shopping with us!" confirmation email comes through.

A few days later, the stuff arrives, its heavy weight transforming it from a digital idea into a real-world problem. But something about it isn't *right*. Whether it's the fit, the shape, or the quality, what's been delivered in that box along with trousers and shoes is disappointment and regret.

Then we start to mind-spin about how this must be an "us" problem. Our body is the problem, we need to lose weight, we're stupid, we can't be trusted. This spirals into another bad day and before we know it, we're back on {insert your retailer of choice} ordering more stuff.

As modern working ways and being on 24/7 take their toll, we've created whole industries out of faux self-care as a way to help us cope. But to quote a popular phrase: self-care is more than taking bubble baths. We use products as plasters, when the wound is weeping and requires anaesthetic, a scalpel, and some serious stitches.

You can't buy your way out of a self-confidence crisis. You may spend all the money on clothes and cosmetic procedures, but the only thing you're changing is your outer shell. Once all the likes have dissipated and the comments have stopped, there you are again, alone with you.

Everywhere you go, there you are. No matter how far you think you're running, or how much you spend on your running equipment, it's a loop taking you back to the same place you began.

Self-care is more than a little treat in the form of a new shirt or pair of shoes. Often, it hurts. It requires dedication and discipline; saying yes to the thing you don't want to do and no to the easy option.

Self-care is taking responsibility for our actions. It's saying no to the easy way out, the dopamine hit, or the 50 per cent off email. It's deleting fashion store apps from our phones and unsubscribing from the emails. It's no longer equating our reliance on consumerism with doing something good for ourselves.

We must fix the system and not the women, and this issue is far bigger than you and your wardrobe can solve. The thing you can do individually, though, that will have a bigger impact than you could comprehend, is addressing the triggers that lead to emotional spending.

You feel like rubbish about your body

Conceptually, we understand that a great outfit has the power to shift how we feel about ourselves. But in the moment, ideals fall away to emotions.

There's a difference between me creating an outfit that feels killer on my curves on a day I feel neutral and unattached, and trying to squeeze myself into an outfit I desperately want to make work, but can't zip up because I'm absolutely full of period rage.

Studies show our bodies fluctuate (thought to be due to water retention) during our menstrual cycles, by around 5lbs.[1] Save that outfit for a day when you'll feel good about it.

You want to "slim into it"

Once again, toxic diet culture raises its malnourished head. Almost every woman has that piece in their wardrobe that's become a stick to beat themselves with. An item to which they equate their self-worth. Overheard in many changing rooms is the line "but if I buy it in this size, it will give me the motivation to lose some weight."

Take it from someone who lost five-and-a-half-stone and whose body image and wardrobe still absolutely sucked: *this top in a smaller size is not the answer to your prayers.* You'd be much better off buying it in a size that fits right now, wearing it, loving life – and you will likely find you make better choices about what to eat and how you respect your body as a side-effect.

---

1. Kanellakis, S. *et al.* (2023) 'Changes in body weight and body composition during the menstrual cycle,' *American Journal of Human Biology,* 35(11), p. e23951. https://doi.org/10.1002/ajhb.23951.

Do this not just for yourself (because it's by being that we become) – but for the person who made it, too.

Did the designer create it so it could stay stuffed in the darkness of your wardrobe for years on end? Did the garment worker toil away to put it together so it could remain indefinitely with the tags on?

Who wins when your focus is diverted to what you weigh, versus what you can do? The diet industry in the UK alone is worth a reported £2billion annually. Globally, it's worth over $31 billion.[2]

Nutrition impacts brain function. Like a lack of fuel means your car would stall, a lack of nutrients can impact your concentration, energy, and even your self-esteem.[3]

You're doing the weekly shop

Can you pick up some trend-led pieces at your local supermarket? Sure. Might there be something there that could suit your personal style and will last you years? Yes. Should you be shopping with so little intention that you're bunging dresses in with your baked beans as you rush round the aisles on your Tuesday lunch break?

I don't believe that buying your clothes during the food shop is the best idea, and every time I've said it, I've been savaged online. Why? Because I'm confronting the society-approved belief that woman is synonymous with martyr.

---

2. Harvard Business School.
3. Selhub, E., MD (2022) *Nutritional psychiatry: Your brain on food*. https://www. health.harvard.edu/blog/nutritional-psychiatry-your-brain-on-food-201511168626.

Picture the scene: You need to do the weekly shop (have you ever considered why *you*, the woman, need to do the weekly shop, even though you're an adult living in a shared home with another adult?) You bundle a screaming child into the trolley; it's got a busted wheel, but before you have a chance to take the child out of the seat and find a new one, your phone pings – it's your boss with another out of hours request. A hot puff of panic pangs in your chest. You feel the urge to reply immediately, because so much of your worth is wrapped up in compliance.

This jogs your memory… you need to get a cake for Susan's birthday and a leaving gift for Mark. Because even though you're the most senior person on your team, you're also the woman, which means pastoral care and organising parties, keeping on top of everyone's birthdays and cleaning up the cake crumbs, has become an unspoken part of your remit. It's not officially in your contract, and there's never any thanks, but there's always an element of disappointment (does it come from them, or is it internal?) when you forget.

You must make sure you get the specific cereal your partner likes, and your toddler is only eating spaghetti hoops right now, and…. ohmygod… where are the spaghetti hoops? You traipse up and down the store trying to find everything, whilst the child grows tired and begins crying, someone with nothing better to do tuts at you like you're a terrible parent because, well, you're a mum so by default, you're doing a terrible job.

Your phone pings again. And again. Missed call from your boss, gaaaah what if you get fired for not answering, even though it's 6pm and… damn, mother-in-law's birthday, must get a card and some flowers. Why? She's not your mother, but it seems as though you entered into a legal obligation to be a surrogate mother to her son, so you're responsible for remembering her birthday. It's never his fault that he doesn't know when it is.

Shittttttttt – the investor meeting is tomorrow. And you have nothing to wear. You've got that one blouse you wear on repeat, but it's looking tired now and last week you spilled your coffee down it. You didn't have time to clean it properly, because of course you're a terrible, lazy waste of space.

You don't feel the same since you had the baby, and what's behind the wardrobe door feels like such an avalanche of emotional baggage you barely have the strength to pull it open.

Somewhere in the back of your mind is the distant memory of before. Before your identity changed, before the pandemic – you kinda, sorta did like getting dressed once-upon-a-time.

Now you're standing paralysed in front of the row of shirts, feeling the immense weight of all this, and maybe if your legs didn't feel so heavy and cemented to the ground, you'd walk right out and keep on walking. But instead, you reach for the generic £15 blouse and put it into the trolley, next to the cat food and the toilet paper.

The next day at your Big Important Meeting, you're in the room, but you're not really in the room. You can't stop focusing on how tight the shoulders on this blouse are, or the way the neckline is scratching your skin. And whilst you think you've done a great job of acting confident and convincing, humans pick up on micro-expressions, body language, and energy. The managing partner/investor/customer gets all the information, but something about the deal just doesn't feel… right. They aren't confident in you, because ultimately you're not confident in yourself.

You've treated yourself with as much value as the bag of potatoes in the trolley next to that £15 shirt.

Women make 85 per cent of all household purchases.[4] A quick trip to the store adds up to hours per week, days across a year. And the supermarkets? They know this. As women have been conditioned to put themselves at the bottom of the pile, of course they might hurriedly shove some clothes in the trolley, because when else is there ever time for them to shop? Especially when shopping for ourselves is labelled selfish and indulgent.

By all means, have a browse in the clothing section at the supermarket if that's your bag. Try on some items at leisure. And that's the point – *at leisure.*

Stylish clothes are accessible at all price-points, but just because something is relatively low-budget doesn't mean it's a bargain. If it's not a match to your personal brand, it doesn't make you feel great, and it's a copy of something else you already own… *what's the point?*

Are you buying it because you love it? Or is it because there's no other time for you? Have you done the pre-work required for a functional wardrobe to warrant this purchase, or is this going to be thrown on the pile inside your closet, to see the light of day once in a blue moon?

If it's just a little treat you're after, there are other things you could buy that don't cost as many planetary resources, or take up so much space. Grab a candle and some bubble bath, and treat yourself to an at-home spa experience. Buy the nice coffee,

---

4. Customer, E. (2024) 'Katie Mares: "Women make 85% of all household purchases",' *Engage Customer*, 19 July. https://www.engagecustomer.com/blog/katie-mares-women-make-85-of-all-household-purchases#:~:text=Women%20in fluence%2043%20trillion%20dollars.

the freshly-baked bread, or some fresh fruit. Not to say these choices do not also cost resources, but in the long-term you are not saddled with another item to find more space for, your house gradually filling with items for which you have no use, and you wondering why you feel stifled.

You know you're avoiding the *actual* work

The deadline for that important presentation is looming and yet suddenly you have the urge to scroll through all 300 "new in" items on the Zara app. You've got to have an awkward conversation… but it can wait until after you've added everything at Asos to your online basket.

I'm writing a book – trust me I understand, and feel viscerally, the urge to procrastinate. It's currently 11pm on a Saturday and here I am tip-tapping away because there's a deadline looming. I'm a former journalist and as one of my peers once said: journalists either want everything six months in advance, or they're working on a deadline that goes to print in 10 minutes, there is no in-between. Whilst I'll happily take the excuse of it being a career hangover, I know what it really is. It's avoidance. Because once this book is out there, it changes everything.

It's all very well me having conceptualised a book. It's all very well me telling people I'm writing a book. But there's a big difference between having one blank page with the title "my book" open on my laptop for three months (true story) and knuckling down, getting it written, and into the hands of the women who need it.

And as excited as I am about the thought of this book in the hands of those women, changing the way they relate to style and freeing them of years of consumerist bullshit, I'm a woman living in the same society as them, so I am not immune to the same stories that stop us all from moving forward.

It's avoidance. And you are using shopping as a "get out" to exit this level of the game. Just when you think the work is going to get you and you're going to have to get up off the sofa and get shit done, aha! The trump card. I've got the distraction of having to buy these clothes right now. And I do have to buy them right now, because signs are flashing up at me saying "40 people are looking at this! Low in stock! You're about to miss out!"

We're not afraid of missing out on the specific item. We're afraid of missing out on becoming the person the item promises we will become if it's in our possession. But it isn't a magic lamp. You've convinced yourself you'll become the person you want to be if you just have that jacket you didn't even know existed until five minutes ago.

Do you know how you'd really become the person you want to be? *By doing the work.*

That might mean simply getting on with it. Having a word with yourself, giving yourself a gentle slap on the cheeks, pouring some coffee, and opening the laptop to the blank page. Or it might mean journaling on why you don't want to get on with it. Or it might mean sticking on some f*ck yes tunes and changing your state, or going for a walk, or dancing in your pants. You'll know what it means for you, but I know what it definitely doesn't: buying another jacket you don't need.

You're going to have spent money you could have invested in stocks and shares and you're still going to have the work to do, with mounting pressure with every second that passes. Does that sound like the actions of the woman you mapped out earlier? We think not.

Let's enhance your fashion education

If the most you know about the inner workings of the fashion industry is re-watching *The Devil Wears Prada,* consider the next chapter your enrolment into style school.

Alexa – play Madonna, Vogue.

Chapter 21

So What are We Really Buying?

You're not buying clothes, you're buying an ideology, and understanding that is how you take your power back.

Love yourself – *if you look like this.*

Love yourself – *not really, but we have to say that or we get backlash.*

Dress for you *wink wink* (that's not *really* what we mean but we can't face another media shitstorm, so we'll put up a little sign with an empty platitude like "love yourself" to offset what we're *actually* saying with our ad campaigns).

In early 2024, Sweaty Betty turned off comments on its social media posts after backlash to its Wear the Damn Shorts campaign. Women felt the slogan would be less contrived coming from a brand that stocks over a size 20. Wear the Damn Shorts – so long as your thighs don't go over a certain circumference. It's a feel-good factor for women who live in bodies deemed acceptable by society. It doesn't advance the cause in a real way, because it's empty, devoid of meaning, fluff.

Heading into the fourth branch of high-street store Reiss in a three-week period, I decided to ask the staff where the clothes over a size 14 are. 'There's just not the demand for over a size 14,' I was told.

'What if those women over a size 14 who would like to shop here *do* actually exist but they've been trained not to come in here because you don't cater to them?' I suggested. She shrugged. Retailers want their cake and to eat it too, when ironically, they don't like women who eat cake.

I went shopping with a long-term client in the height of summer. The first place we began overhauling her wardrobe was underwear. The underwear drawer is generally the most neglected part of a wardrobe because it's just for us (except when it's sold on the idea of sex, which we'll come onto in a second) but it can make a big difference to the fit and feel of your clothes.

We're so used to style as performance that upgrading our wardrobe is usually done when it relates to the way others see us: an event we have to go to, an important business trip. The next time you are about to drop hard-earned cash on random items in a "fuck I have nothing to wear to this party" panic – put it towards your foundations.

As my client was being fitted for a new bra at a well-known women's underwear store, something jarred with me in the waiting area. On one wall was a huge sign in handwritten script that said "look good, feel great, [your body is] something to celebrate." On the opposite wall hung a huge TV screen playing the latest ad campaign on a loop. The models were in swimwear, shot in some far-flung location. There was no body diversity whatsoever in the entire three-minute sequence. Long, lean limbs stretching from sand to sky. Washboard abs and super perky boobs. Women rolling around on sun-loungers giving eyes to the camera. I felt confused and conflicted looking from one wall, telling me to love myself, to the other, showing me all the ways my body is wrong.

The ad campaign was clearly made for the male gaze – meaning media that's created from the viewpoint of a heterosexual male. But even to call it *that* seems insulting to men. We're being sold an idea of what men are being told they want us to be, as opposed to what they really want us to be, and most importantly, what we want for ourselves.

Film theorist Laura Mulvey theorises that "the male gaze limits the possibilities for the female spectator imagining herself as a woman with agency, on the one hand, and escaping identifying herself as a passive object, on the other."[1] In other words, you want control over how you're perceived and how you perceive yourself, but you're also conditioned to objectify yourself.

Between those two walls – the idea that you can love yourself as you are, and that how you are is not good enough – is where women exist. The energy of simply turning your head from one wall to the other, trying to figure out which is the direction you want to go, is exhausting.

Aspiration is the cornerstone of sales psychology, but there's a difference between me *aspiring* to have a swimming costume that makes me feel amazing in the body I have right now, and a campaign built on aesthetics that are out of reach for 99 per cent of the female population.

You exist suspended between the belief that you too could be that model, writhing around carefree in make up that has not, by some miracle, sweated off – and knowing this could never realistically be you – but wanting a piece of it anyway.

---

1. Oliver, K. (2017) 'The male gaze is more relevant, and more dangerous, than ever,' *New Review of Film and Television Studies*, 15(4), pp. 451–455. https://doi.org/10.1080/17400309.2017.1377937.

Now, with the rise of AI models, like those used in a 2025 Guess campaign in American *Vogue*, it is not enough to compare yourself to other *human* women. Now you are competing with robots. And whilst logically you know that there is not a woman alive who looks like this on the beach (not even the human models in the campaign), emotionally – you can't help yourself. You're suckered in. For just long enough for you to hand your credit card over, the fantasy stays vivid in your mind.

Maybe I could look like that if I just starved myself between now and my holiday? Maybe I could get that toned if I went to the gym twice a day?

You forget for a minute all about your very real, big, busy life with lots of responsibilities which mean it would be logistically impossible for you to gym twice a day, and which also requires you to intake enough calories so that you can fulfil all said responsibilities.

The unrealistic standards set by advertising ruin women's self-confidence and warp men's understanding of what female bodies look like. It also turns women against women. We judge the models, we make assumptions about their intelligence. We *other* women we perceive as more physically attractive than ourselves.

Parts of our bodies were demonised so beauty and fashion companies could sell us products.

Let's start with one of the worst scourges of women's bodies of all time: cellulite. Except cellulite doesn't exist. Subcutaneous fat and fibrous tissue exist. These are a normal part of the anatomy of all people, not just women. The original definition of "cellulite" is tissue cells in a state of inflammation or infection. But in 1968, *Vogue* – a magazine that makes money from advertising – used the term to describe perfectly normal subcutaneous fat. Then its advertisers (large corporations in the beauty industry) were able to sell products to generations of women promising to help us defeat the scourge of cellulite.

Did you know that until the 1910s, women were all good with their body hair? But Gillette realised it could only sell to half the population, so it came out with a lady razor and advertised in magazines.[2]

And then, of course, there's the pink tax – a toll on women that sees them paying around 20 per cent more for the same products as men. They tell us these products are *essential… and charge us more for the privilege of having them.*

Adverts often depict idealised versions of reality, which can lead to unrealistic expectations about the outcomes of products. But you *know* that already. You're an intelligent consumer, you're logically aware that this bikini, or cellulite cream, or new fangled next-gen product, does not fundamentally change your body. So what is it that *really* makes you want to buy?

It's a matcha-flavoured concoction of wanting acceptance, assimilation, and self-actualisation.

We are buying ideology, not just clothes

Research shows displays of luxury consumption prompt favourable behaviour towards the wearer.[3] One experiment on

2. Berkowitz, A., PhD (2020) 'Many risky methods have been employed in Western societies to destroy body hair.,' *Psychology Today*, 6 July. https://www.psychologytoday.com/gb/blog/governing-behavior/202007/femininitys-war-against-body-hair.
3. Nelissen, R. M. A., & Meijers, M. H. C. (2011) 'Social benefits of luxury brands

status perception involved having participants wear either a Lacoste or Tommy Hilfiger shirt, as compared with a non-brand-labeled shirt. Those wearing the brand-labeled shirt were perceived as wealthier and of higher status.

In another experiment, researchers had someone with a clipboard approach shoppers and request they complete a survey. When the person with clipboard was wearing a clearly-branded T-shirt, shoppers complied 52.2 per cent of the time, compared with 13 per cent of the time for the person in the non-branded T-shirt.

In a 2020 study on Zoom style, people wearing labelled versus unlabelled clothes were perceived as more competent.

People treat the same person differently when they wear branded items.

Do we make ourselves the brand, or do we make the brand what it is?

What's interesting is how further research indicates that we as women judge other women based on the quality and brand of our clothes – and there is a negative correlation between wearing labels and likeability. One study showed women who wore luxury items were viewed by women as younger, more ambitious, and more attractive and flirty... but also less loyal, smart and mature.[4]

I know you're frustrated by your experiences, conflicting pressures, and unrealistic expectations. And after a lifetime of

---

as costly signals of wealth and status.' *Evolution and Human Behavior*, 32(5), 343–355. https://doi.org/10.1016/j.evolhumbehav.2010.12.002

4. Hudders, L. *et al.* (2014) 'The rival wears Prada: Luxury Consumption as a female competition strategy,' *Evolutionary Psychology*, 12(3), pp. 570–587. https://doi.org/10.1177/147470491401200306.

wasted energy and mental torture at the hands of retailers, you're likely thinking, 'Nah, I'll just give up! Where's the nearest nudist encampment?'

There is another way (that doesn't involve freezing your boobs off).

We are buying ideology, not clothes. The shops we choose to align ourselves with say something about our beliefs and the world we want to live in.

This book is about how to take your power – and our collective power – back. I don't want you to feel like you have to choose to shop online only from companies that are so embarrassed by you they refuse to host you in-store. I want you to remember that, as the customer, *you* get to direct where your money goes. Might this mean a more inconvenient experience – having clothing tailor made, searching preloved, investigating what your favourite stores stand for? Yes. But you can disengage with anyone or anything that makes you feel like shit. You get to ask yourself, at the point of handing over your credit card: *what am I really buying?*

Just Get Dressed: End of chapter task

Get out your notebook again and answer the following:

- How do I make purchasing decisions?
- Can I pinpoint a product I bought based on the idea of who I could be?
- Can I pinpoint the emotional drivers that lead me to a purchase?
- Where and when have I outsourced my results to products in the past?

- List out your priorities about where you spend. E.g. is local important to you? Sustainability? Convenience? Trends? (There is no right or wrong, this is about self-awareness).

Chapter 22

Fuck You, Jane Norman

That iconic pink bag has a lot to answer for.

Secondary school can be a hellish experience for teenage girls. And if the sight of *that* pink Jane Norman bag triggers your olfactory senses into a choke-worthy haze of *Charlie Red*, I can tell why you're now a grown woman with a wardrobe you kinda hate. You feel like you're going to be *Mean Girl*-ed, as if this is all a practical joke, like the time you got locked in Jenny Bradfield's cupboard at her 13th birthday party.

Growing up in any era is tough, all those hormones and bodily changes, trying to figure out who you are and what you want to do with your life. But the evolution of social media has brought about a whole extra set of problems for anyone Millennial or younger. Our first computer was in nursery, or earlier, meaning life has been plugged in since before clear memory.

Is it any wonder that Millennial women have the lowest body confidence of any generation?[1]

Our youth collided with red-top newspapers, gossip magazines that drew big rings around celebrity body parts and ranked them best and worst in bikinis each year, mothers on Weight Watchers and the Special K diet. That's right, we hit puberty right as a

---

1. https://www.dove.com/ca/en/stories/campaigns/global-state-of-beau ty.html

cereal brand devised a meal plan out of cereal and freeze-dried berries.

And as if the evidence of "your body is disgusting" was not all around you in the physical world, (every time your mother picked at her non-existent belly fat in the mirror, or you walked into the corner shop to see Jessica Simpson, a perfectly healthy woman, splashed across the cover of a newspaper under some awful headline) – the internet added toxic diet culture and harmful body stereotypes to your awareness times a trillion.

As I wrote in the previous chapter, brands use clothing to signal status. For many women, this starts young, with something as simple as a pink bag. The Jane Norman bag was a statement: *I'm thin enough to buy here.* Because before Zara tried to tell women a size 12 is extra large, there was Jane Norman – and it felt like she was even more ruthless.

I was not thin enough for Jane Norman. In fact during my university days I was turned down for a job there. I do not have definitive proof it was down to my size, but I felt the cold, judgemental stare of the interviewing manager and wondered why the hell I hadn't cancelled. Just as well, the brand went bust in 2011 closing all of its 89 stores.[2]

I think I only wanted to work there – much like why I started my career in magazines – because I thought it meant something about my validity as a woman. If I could be accepted here, then I wasn't the hideous monster these brands, ironically, had made me feel I was. I would be in the door, no longer peering in through the windows and doing all sorts of weird shit to punish my body into becoming Jane Norman-acceptable.

---

2. BBC News (2011) *Fashion chain Jane Norman goes into administration.* https://www.bbc.co.uk/news/business-13926277.

For many a 40-something or 30-something woman, the sight of that pink carrier bag brings back the "I'm not good enough" feeling. This is because clothes have meaning far beyond keeping us *clothed*. They are psychological tools rather than material items, and labels carry meaning as well as a heftier price tag (or physical pain). If you can afford to buy the item and you can fit into it – it says something about you. And as a result, your status improves.

The double bind

In July 2025, I posted on LinkedIn about a client with a £250,000 salary who found herself digging through the sale rack at Marks and Spencer when she wanted to dress in Max Mara. In this book, we've covered numerous pieces of research that show the way a woman dresses is still used as an indicator of her leadership skills and success. My client realised how old stories about money and clothing were impacting her ability to dress to the level of her new role, and this was in turn impacting how she was perceived.

In sharing this story, I was subjected to a litany of negativity from other women – telling me how silly, dumb, and vain we both were. The idea that women can't be both smart and stylish holds us back, but it's *us* perpetuating the myth. We hold one another in a state of collective female martyrdom, because that's how we are most likeable.

Studies have shown that "when women asserted their ideas, made direct requests and advocated for themselves, they were judged as less hireable."[3] Society expects women to be warm,

____

3. Williams, M. J., & Tiedens, L. Z. (2016) 'The subtle suspension of backlash: A meta-analysis of penalties for women's implicit and explicit dominance

selfless, and nurturing, and punishes them when they break these stereotypes.

Chujun Lin, an assistant professor of psychology at the University of California, San Diego suggests there are two parts to likeability. Speaking to *The Guardian*, she said: "One is what you see," [like someone's appearance or mannerisms] "but the other is based on the template I already have in my mind, like prejudice or stereotypes." These are dubbed "bottom up" and "top down" assessments, respectively. And in practice, these two can combine in ways that disadvantage certain groups.

The weird thing about the Jane Norman bag? I never perceived anyone who had one as likeable. My judgement certainly marries up with the research, showing that we see women with status symbols as less smart or kind. But then, I *was* bullied by girls who had those bags – so my association is: Jane Norman equals mean girl. And it's important to remember our experiences of a brand, whilst collective through the way it markets itself, are also individual.

In the USA, Brandy Melville was the cool brand to be wearing, and in a documentary about the downfall of the company, one female shopper recounts buying the iconic star necklace all her friends at high school were wearing. She recalls thinking the girls [who didn't wear Brandy Melville] "weren't as great as I was; maybe they weren't as pretty, maybe there was something wrong with them."[4]

It's also important to note how whiteness was a key ingredient in what's in and out. As one Black former employee told the

---

behavior.' *Psychological Bulletin*, 142(2), 165–197. https://doi.org/10.1037/bul0000039
4. *Brandy Hellville & The Cult of Fast Fashion*, Lightbox, HBO Documentary Films, 2024.

camera, non-white people worked behind the scenes and "if you're white [...] you're in sight."

"We all knew it was not right that [black employees] were pushed in the back out of sight."

I've never spoken to Jane Norman. I don't think she's a real person. But did the brand set out to be Mean Girl Cult Status, and thus choose its font, colour palette, sizing, and staff accordingly? Or did one It Girl put her coursework into that carrier bag one day without much thought and create a moment that reverberated around high schools up and down the land?

How did this happen pre-social media? One weekend, two cousins who went to different schools were discussing the latest happenings, and one mentioned to the other that carrying your PE kit in a Jane Norman bag was the hot thing, now? In a piece for *Vice*, one nostalgic shopper says: "At school, you'd look to the girls in the year or two above to see what was cool."[5]

When we buy labels, we buy meaning. A young woman acquiring a piece of vintage Jane Norman today isn't truly hankering after a badly-fitting roll-neck. She is seeking to acquire the qualities she perceives of the brand's typical shopper. In this case, older, cooler, and more confident. But do we align ourselves with the brand values, or do we make the brand what it ultimately becomes?

Can a designer ever claim true ownership of an item they created, or is the creative process as much about the wearer? For a brand, or an item, to become "it" there has to be buy-in from someone. Thus "what's hot" is more of a partnership between brand and shopper.

---

5. Wilson, S. and Wilson, S. (2024) *The Rise, Fall and Rise Again of Jane Norman.* https://www.vice.com/en/article/jane-norman-depop-2000s-revival/.

At the time of writing, Jane Norman is enjoying (though she doesn't know it bless her, she's dead) a resurgence in popularity with Gen Z who are nostalgic about 00's skinny, likely because they weren't there and don't understand how toxic it was. It's interesting to look at how this rise in skinny chic correlates with economic uncertainty and a rise in far-right politics.

Starve the women, then they won't be able to think.

Just Get Dressed: End of chapter task

Pick one status symbol from your youth and unpick your story about it.

- Did you possess this status symbol?
- At the time, what did you feel like it meant about you – to have it or not?
- What is your relationship with brands and labels today?
- How do you think your relationships with brands and labels as a youth has impacted your relationships with brands and labels into adulthood?
- What beliefs do you carry (and get them out, without self-judgement) about women who wear labels or designer?
- How have you judged yourself for your own relationship with labels?

Chapter 23

Trends vs Style

You don't have to choose; you can weave trends into your style without losing yourself or your money to the hype.

I've been repping the leopard since people were calling me Bet Lynch and Kat Slater (UK soap-star legends). Leopard print was never *not* going to be on the cover of this book. And at the time of writing, it's *everywhere*. You could go so far as to say it's been overdone as a trend, to the point where it's a neutral.

I don't care – I'll be doing leopard print and big hair, bordering on a Janice-from-*Friends* impression, until the day I die. I remember being around 12 years old and really, really wanting a faux-fur leopard print coat. At this point, leopard print was in its obsolescence. When I got one for Christmas (my mum never shared my love of style, she would look at me with bemusement whenever I went off foraging through charity shops or poring through fashion editorials), I felt like a glorious cross between a fabulous drag queen and a 1920s starlet. I probably looked like the Gruffalo.

That's the power of fashion; we get to try on different personalities and figure out who we are.

We get to embody – thanks to our friend enclothed cognition – the characteristics we want to amp up.

It likely won't surprise you that right now, typing this chapter, I am wearing a leopard-print shirt and shorts co-ord. *Hot Stuff* by Donna Summer is blaring through my speakers because, well, this is the enduring power of leopard print.

But how do you figure out if something *is* enduring, or just a passing phase? And is it OK to buy into a passing phase? And is it really trends versus style, or can you have both? Search this last question on the internet and you'll find loads of content arguing the case for one over the other. I believe in the power of both.

Firstly, as you'll discover in these next pages, there really is no such thing as dead when it comes to fashion. Almost every single thing hanging in your wardrobe is inspired by something of the past.

Secondly, everything started as a trend once. Certain items became enduring, but it took one person to wear them first, risking the ridicule of their peers, and for someone else to go, 'That looks cool, I'm going to try it.'

Knowledge is power. The clearer you are on how this stuff works, the better the decisions you'll make, the more confident you'll feel, and no one – not a snarky sales assistant or some arsehole on social media – can make you feel less than.

Besides, how can you keep feeling fresh and look like the most innovative person your industry has ever seen if you're exclusively stuck in "classic" and you don't know how to move your look forward?

Let's demystify how trends work

The concept of "trends" is thought to have emerged in the 14th Century, when the upper echelons of society were showing off about how quickly they could afford to change their looks.

Trends were commercialised from the early 1700s, after Louis XIV introduced rules requiring textile designers to produce fabrics and styles twice a year, for winter and summer. As explained in *The Times*:

> "The aim wasn't only to boost their sales. By forcing the French nobility to spend enormous sums on the latest products, Louis kept them in a state of perpetual debt, dependent on royal pensions and too poor to fund a rebellion. Consumers have shelled out for the latest looks since."[1]

For a long time, the trend cycle (the time it takes for a trend to peak, decline, and re-emerge) was thought to be 20 years. This was proven by science in 2026, when professors at Northwestern University used spectral analysis spot patterns in popular styles. But as fashion production cycles got faster and faster, many professionals believe it's now a much shorter cycle. And even the data from the study shows that trends are now more fragmented, with multiple ones existing simultaneously, versus one dominant trend.

Traditionally, we had the spring/summer and autumn/winter fashion weeks, which fashion editors could use to plan what

---

1. Blakely, R. (2026) 'Don't throw out that dress — it'll be back in fashion in 20 years,' *The Times*, 17 March. https://www.thetimes.com/uk/science/article/fashion-20-year-rule-ndvxcs32j.

would be coming in for the next year. Then came mini-collections like "resortwear"... and now manufacturing clothes is so quick that we've got new collections coming out practically every week.

Trends are usually a reflection of a changing cultural mood. For example, during the pandemic and immediately after, dopamine dressing was big news. It coincided with our kitchen discos and our need for a creative outlet when we could only leave our homes for one hour a day.

This is the thing about trends. You've been looking to fashion for a steer on what's hot, when the big secret is: fashion looks to the street to gauge the trends. It's one of the biggest rackets. They're looking at what we're wearing, or talking about, or being influenced by in a micro-way (examples these days might be a Netflix show), then selling it back to us under the guise that it's new!!!

Trends in fashion aren't simply whatever some designer made up in their head; they're more complicated than that and they're influenced by the zeitgeist.

But the irony is that to be on-trend, you really need to get to the trend before it *becomes* the trend. (Confused yet? Bear with me!) Let's say you're starting to notice ties making a comeback. Wearing this accessory could be classed a micro-trend but you know it's going to be big this autumn-winter. You've noticed some of your favourite style icons sporting ties, maybe you've seen them on the women in your favourite TV shows.

The three types of trend

There are three types of trend – repeat, major, and micro.

Repeat trends are things we see return over and over again. Think of that scene in *The Devil Wears Prada*, when Miranda Priestly says, 'Florals for spring? How groundbreaking.' These trends often have seasonality and mimic nature. In autumn, for example, we see lots of dark greens, moody florals, and dark gothic themes in the clothing on offer. At Christmas, there's a party mood – sequins, velvet, pizzaz.

Buy once, look after it, and you can be on trend year after year without contributing any further to fashion's toxic overproduction. And because these repeat trends are literally repeated year after year, you don't even need to buy new. You'll find thousands of preloved options.

Major trends could be something like western, which has been all over the place for the last couple of years, thanks in part to Beyoncé's country-themed music, the style of pop culture figures like Sabrina Carpenter, and acclaimed TV shows like *Yellowstone*. In 2023, Barbiecore was a peak hot-trend thanks to the release of the movie. Major trends have a shorter lifespan than repeats because they're not popping up year after year, but they speak to a specific moment in time.

I bet if you heard a certain song, it would take you back to a particular time in your mind. I bet if you pull a particular item of clothing from your closet, it would have the same effect.

Then there are **micro-trends**. Generally these are two-fold:

1. An off-shoot of a bigger, longer-lasting trend.
2. Accessories or a way of wearing something specific.

Both are more niche and are likely to be adopted by those who consider themselves to have their fingers on the pulse of fashion.

A real-world example – giant bows on shoes. These were shown by Loewe in the fall 2022 collection during Paris Fashion Week.[2] Social media went wild for them, retailers picked up on it, and soon versions were everywhere from Sam Edelman to Asos to Zara.

The trend lifecycle

The trend lifecycle has five stages.

1. The **introduction**. This is usually the first time we see something – like a colour or a silhouette – on the runway, or on a celebrity.
2. After introduction comes **rise** – this is when the trend gets traction. As celebrities and influencers start dressing to the trend (sometimes they have paid partnerships), consumer demand increases and mass-market brands start producing versions.
3. **Peak** is the saturation point – this is when the trend reaches the height of its popularity. It might seem like it's everywhere. One example you might remember – the £40 spotty Zara dress from summer 2019. It even had its own Instagram account.[3]
4. Sooner or later, the trend goes into **decline**. The trend has

---

2. *Runway · Fall-Winter 2022 women's collection · LOEWE* (no date). https://www.loewe.com/eur/en/stories-collection/fw22-women-runway.html.

3. Kale, S. (2019) 'The story of The Dress: how a £40 Zara frock stole the summer,' *The Guardian*, 21 August. https://www.theguardian.com/lifeandstyle/2019/aug/11/the-story-of-the-dress-how-a-40-zara-frock-stole-the-summer.

become accessible to the masses to the point where it's no longer aspirational.

5. And the final phase is **obsolescence** – it's well and truly over and we want to forget we ever met!

A trend can last for an indeterminate amount of time. It's not like there's a fashion police and after six months of a trend going hardcore, they come along and round up anyone still wearing that thing. But trend-forecasting is a muscle you can build.

We want you to be seen as fresh, innovative, and the right person to lead into the future. If you can hit a trend during rise, not peak, by the time it has mass-market appeal, everyone you know will be saying: "[your name] did it first" – cementing your status as a fashion icon.

Keeping on top of what looks modern now should be something you view as a business activity. If this doesn't come naturally to you, just like flexing a muscle at the gym, put in the time to practice. Many of my clients work in industries such as tech and finance and they often think of themselves as analytical without much creativity. I'm the opposite. So just like I put time in my diary to learn about tech, or keep on top of my finances, I advise them to put some time in their diaries to look at style.

I think style has the power to help us maintain our vitality. Look at someone like Iris Apfel as an example. She lived to be 102 and she was dressing to the nines on the daily. She wasn't going, 'Oh now I've reached [this age] I'd better fade into the background and pretend I don't exist.'

The key for trends you've seen before is to keep them fresh. You likely don't want to look like you're going to a costume party, but it doesn't mean you can't dabble. **That said, even classics change over time.**

A blazer is always in style. It's in the "classic" category. It's a symbol of formality. It can level up a casual outfit for a smarter occasion, as well as perform the function of keeping you warm. But just because something is timeless doesn't mean the specific version of that item you own is.

If you took a blazer made in the 1980s and held it against a blazer from the current year, you'd see some major differences.

It might be that the 1980s blazer – constructed before the rise of fast fashion – is of better quality. Likely your vintage blazer would have lining and facing. Depending on the price point of a modern version, you may be unlikely to see the same quality or the same amount of inner construction. Lining and facing not only help garments sit better, they protect from wear and tear, especially in areas that might typically rub, like underarms.

Back in the 1980s you likely could have paid a moderate price for a blazer that would look pretty decent today. Unless you're dropping upwards of £300 on a blazer today, it probably won't look as good, or even be in a wearable condition, in 40 years' time.

Aside from the quality, there are differences in shape and cut. If the 1980s conjure images of massive perms and even bigger shoulder pads, then what do you think the shape of a jacket from the time would be? Whilst jackets made now have shoulder pads, you're likely not going to see anything quite so extreme for everyday dressing.

Jeans are another classic that change shape over time. Denim has staying power, but the way we wear changes. From super skinny, to wide leg, the cut of your jeans can say a lot about you. Not least how long it took you to put them on (don't tell me I am the only one who ever got stuck in a pair of Topshop Joni's).

It's a trend checklist

Use this list of questions to help you "read" what you see on the runways. You'll feel like a *Vogue* correspondent in no time!

1. Fashion is a mirror to the climate – so what is going on right now in worldwide events, popular culture, and public discourse that may influence what comes down the catwalk?
2. What colours do I see on repeat? What are the pervasive neutrals of the season? (Black, brown, nude, grey, oxblood, khaki?)
3. What shapes keep coming up? Are things oversized or fitted? Tailored, slim, or exaggerated? Extreme or conservative?
4. Is there reference to a specific historic era, or overarching style of dress? (For example, western or bohemian).
5. What lengths do I notice? Short, maxi, midi?
6. Are there any patterns, prints or materials that keep making an appearance?
7. If I were to name a celebrity, fictional character, or person who would look right at home in these trends, who would it be?
8. If I were to pick three to four keywords for the mood of the upcoming season, what would they be?

The tiers of fashion

What is the difference between a designer label and haute couture? As a summary you can remember – as the tiers get lower, the price reduces, the stock increases, and they have more mass appeal.

Haute couture – think rare, one-off, specialist. Price: unlimited. Stock: extremely limited and likely one-of-a-kind. This is where fine craftsmanship meets art. There's a reason Parisians argue their city is the fashion capital of the world; the label "haute couture" enjoys legal protection.

To qualify, brands must own an atelier in Paris, employ more than 15 full-time employees and exhibit at least 35 looks a year, twice yearly. Recognised by the *Fédération de la Haute Couture et de la Mode* in Paris, only a select number of designers are permanent members, including Chanel, Christian Dior, Givenchy, and Maison Margiela.

There's an important distinction between haute and not. Couture can refer to any hand-made, one-of-a-kind garment. The *haute* is bestowed on brands by the federation.

Designer and luxury – these generally set the trends and determine what will be trickling down through the rest of the fashion chain over the course of the next year to 18 months. Their latest concepts are displayed on runaways at fashion week twice yearly and translated by magazines, street style content creators, and stylists for the general masses. Designer and luxury fashion usually retains its value.

Contemporary – you know that girl you knew at school who was always effortlessly cool but never a slave to trends? This is the persona of the contemporary fashion brand. The Frankie Shop, for example, was doing killer waistcoats before they went viral (but not before Gareth Southgate, let's give him his due). Ganni is known for its distinctive leopard print and edgy sports-luxe vibe. This is not at the same price point as traditional designer, but nevertheless it still feels like an investment.

Accessible luxury and diffusion – this is the cheaper line from a designer brand which likely would not be in the same store as that other stuff. The idea of this is not simply to make designer clothing accessible. It's quite clever really: get the money of the masses, but make it clear they aren't getting the real deal. Keep a barrier between them and the real customers – the ones who are of the aesthetic and financial means the brands like to associate with. I generally advise my clients to steer clear of diffusion if they're looking to elevate their style for a higher position or well-paying client.

Working with a personal stylist isn't something people are generally public about, but stylish people often do. If you're talking to a successful business woman with a strong personal brand who always looks vibey as fuck, the likelihood is she works with a stylist. She has taken the time to educate herself in this arena, because she understands it's a business investment. She can spot diffusion a mile off.

I think you're better off saving up and investing in the real deal which holds its value a lot better and can even increase in value if it's the right item.

Premium high street – the level above the mass. For example, & Other Stories, which is the "big sister" of H&M. She's of a slightly higher quality, sometimes more directional, and costs about three times as much.

Mass (this is fast fashion) – the brands you'll find on the high street. Some, fair play, are "does what it says it does"; others like to pretend they're not what they are. They're the brand equivalent to those personal brand gurus you see on LinkedIn who amass loads of followers and carry an air that they're better than the rest of us, when underneath there's absolutely nothing of substance.

Style doesn't come from exclusively wearing designer (that just makes you a clothes horse, not someone with creativity). The best kind of outfits are the ones that mix tiers, trends, and style references to create something totally unique.

Fast fashion makes new trends accessible for us mere mortals, but it causes problems for designers. Smaller designers often report being ripped off by the big brands. A fast fashion brand has the infrastructure to not only look at the runway and replicate designs within days, it can do the same to independents at the bottom of the ladder without the capital behind them to sue.

Ultrafast fashion – unfortunately our journey into the tiers of style doesn't end at "fast." Fast isn't fast enough these days. We gotta be ULTRA fast. If "add to basket" was an Olympic sport, there'd be a serious number of contenders. To give you the perspective of how fast fashion has become, H&M launches more than 4,000 items per collection. Shein releases around 10,000 items per day.[4]

Consumers aren't buying clothes to wear, they're buying clothes for content creation.[5] The United States and Europe are consuming around 36 billion units of clothing a year, and 85 per cent of those get discarded.[6]

---

4. NielsenIQ (2025) *Shein, Zara, H&M: Close-up on the Ultra-Fast Fashion Market - NIQ.* https://nielseniq.com/global/en/insights/analysis/2023/shein-zara-hm-close-up-on-the-ultra-fast-fashion-market/.
5. Shadel, J. (2025) *What is Ultra Fast Fashion? Investigating Why It's Ultra Bad - Good On You.* https://goodonyou.eco/ultra-fast-fashion/.
6. *Brandy Hellville & The Cult of Fast Fashion*, Lightbox, HBO Documentary Films, 2024.

How to use these tiers to elevate your style

In *The Big Leap*, Gay Hendricks talks about "the upper limit problem." This suggests we all have a cap on what we think we're worth. There will be certain brands and places that feel too much for you. Go through the tiers of style and consider where that limit exists in your life. There will be brands that right now, you don't fuck with, because you think they're above you. You hurry by them, side-eyeing the door staff as if you're under suspicion. Maybe you build up the courage to take a peek inside, but feel like you've done something wrong the minute the shop assistant says a cheery "good morning!" And that's a problem for your income. If there are shops you count yourself out of, then by extension you're counting yourself out of the income level where you'd be comfortable buying there.

Style elevation is not an overnight change of appearance, it's gradual. Your comfort zone level of shops will, in a while, be two or three up from where you perceive yourself now. Find your comfort zone tier – the one at which you're buying the most. Then look at the tier above and select one brand from that tier which speaks to your ideal style. Bookmark the website. Commit to a regular scroll. Find the nearest bricks-and-mortar store, or concession, and go for a visit. Dress up and be the woman who belongs there.

Set up eBay alerts and see if you can invest in a piece, or accessory, that you'll wear regularly to reap the benefits of enclothed cognition.

Duped by the dupes

You're wearing a cool pair of flats that you picked up last week in a high street store. They're a bit different, right? Except… they're a designer rip-off.

You just don't know they are. Unless you are wearing a one-off design, everything in your wardrobe is a direct copy of, or inspired by, something else. Dupes are becoming more and more like the real thing in terms of design, thanks to emerging technologies that speed up the manufacturing process.

So if you want your wardrobe to look quality – and support you in business – it's worth keeping your finger on the pulse and understanding where the idea for your new shoes actually came from. Maybe they aren't so new after all. Then when someone says,"'Omg is that the bag from the [designer brand] 2021?" you can be like… *hair flick* "No but I absolutely know what you're talking about."

So many people believe themselves to be above the conversation about fashion trends, ignorant that they're wearing something modelled on a very specific designer concept. Sure, a trained stylist can see the difference between the high street flats you picked up for £30 and the £2,000 designer version. But likely most people wouldn't know, right? So what does it matter?

One study found that men wearing a bespoke suit were perceived to be more confident and have a higher salary than men wearing off-the-rack.[7] This shows that regardless of previous knowledge of style (participants ranged in age from 18-

---

7. Howlett, N. *et al.* (2013) 'The influence of clothing on first impressions,' *Journal of Fashion Marketing and Management*, 17(1), pp. 38–48. https://doi.org/10.1108/13612021311305128.

67 in a range of jobs), we have an innate ability to read someone's outfit. Damhorst (1990) states that "dress is a systematic means of transmission of information about the wearer."

Whilst at first glance, the shoes might look very similar to the designer pair, there will be differences in the craftsmanship, colour, and hardware that give the game away. Look out for:

- Seams and stitching. Really give it a good tug! How even and straight is the stitching? Are there any raw or unfinished hems, and are these part of the design, or a cost-cutting measure? How well are the buttons attached? And does it come with spares (that you will actually store away somewhere safely, that you remember the location of)?
- Materials. Retailers have some real nifty PR-spin ways of saying "new plastics" these days. Faux anything normally means plastic.
- Hardware and accessories. Check the zips – I've seen many a cheap zip ruin a great skirt. Also check the heels of your shoes – do they appear well-constructed, or are they finished with cheap plastic that will pop off the bottom of the heel and break the rest of it?
- When you buy a dress that comes with its own tie, or a pair of trousers with a free belt, those are almost always cut-offs of cheap material and they can ruin the feel of the whole look. Replace these with your own accessories, and your outfit will have the added bonus of being you.

Fake it 'til you make it?

What about *knowingly* wearing a fake? Can you get the same feeling of status from a rip-off as the real deal? Research suggests otherwise. A Harvard Business School study showed that wearing counterfeit products makes individuals feel less authentic and "increases their likelihood of both behaving dishonestly and judging others as unethical."

In four experiments, participants wore purportedly fake or authentically branded sunglasses. Those wearing fake sunglasses cheated more across multiple tasks than did participants wearing authentic sunglasses. Researchers said the effects of wearing counterfeit items "extend beyond the self, influencing judgments of other people's unethical behavior." They also concluded that people underestimate the impact of wearing fakes on ethicality, meaning whilst we think we are saving money or have got ourselves a good deal, we underestimate the true cost of wearing them.[8]

Get over "I want it now"

Never before has it been so easy to get what you want in an instant.

Before we go any further, let's make the distinction between want and need. To need an item is to require it for survival, function, or because not having it hinders life experience. To want an item is to understand it's not essential or necessary, but might enhance your life in some way.

8. Gino, F. and Norton, M. (2010) 'The Counterfeit Self: the Deceptive Costs of Faking It,' *ACR North American Advances* [Preprint]. https://www.acrwebsite. org/volumes/v37/acr_v37_15240.pdf.

In this Age of Influence, the number of items you think you need is getting higher and higher. It's more important than ever to understand the distinction between want and need. And if you do acknowledge wanting something, and that is enough for you to have it, you need to get over the feeling you must have it *now*.

I've recently had two bags made to order from an independent designer. She sent me updates all the way through the making process. I chose the materials, sizes, and clasps. I was involved in every step, which made me appreciate the process. Because it took time, I had prepared how I'd wear them. When the bags arrived, I knew I was going to use them and treasure them for a long time. Every time I use them I get comments. They mean something to me. I look at them and see the work, both the work I did to afford them, and the fine craftsmanship of the maker.

We have forgotten how to wait. And that's ironic for the English, where queuing is such an integral part of our genetics, we have a queue guide for Wimbledon.

In a world of 24/7 messaging, same-day delivery, and on-demand access to entertainment, waiting hasn't become just a nuisance, it's almost intolerable. But what if you could view waiting as an enticing part of the purchasing process?

Let's borrow the desire to wait from younger generations, who were born in the age of instant-access and are reporting increased levels of anxiety and depression as a result. A study for the *New York Times* showed that 68 per cent of Gen Z feel nostalgic for eras before their lifetime.[9] Over 80 per cent wish it

---

9. Routledge, C. (2024) 'Why Gen Z Is Resurrecting the 1990s.' *The New York Times*, 24 August, www.nytimes.com/2025/08/24/opinion/gen-z-technology-nostalgia.html

was easier to be unplugged, and the majority believe technology drives people apart and increases anxiety.

'I can't believe this!' my 17-year-old sister-in-law said as we perused the rails of a vintage store. Leather jackets from the 1980s, good-as-new fur jackets from the 1960s, a beautiful briefcase, a silk waistcoat, and printed ties. The quality was far superior than what is being manufactured today – and the items had clearly been taken care of with an appreciation for clothing that's long been forgotten.

I felt all at once excited about our finds – and sad that decades from now, there will likely be no vintage, because our instant-gratification has, in part, become responsible for a major decline in the quality of clothing.

My sister-in-law told me that she had an item on order from a small independent manufacturer, and that the wait was part of her reason for purchasing. Whilst my generation might pay more for quicker delivery… hers will pay more to wait.

Chapter 24

How to Shop

A 9-step guide to shopping like you really mean it.

No rules, no prescriptions. Just a gal who's navigated everything we've covered and knows a thing or two about clothes. Follow the whole thing from start to finish, borrow parts of this process, or sack it off completely if you like.

Step One: The wardrobe assessment

Each season, I assess how well I can stylishly navigate what's coming. If you're reading a book like this, you're probably a bit of a self-development junkie. You will absolutely have changed and evolved since this season came around last year. Therefore, it's important your wardrobe matches your future, not your past.

If you have evolved, it's likely your style has evolved, or needs to. Whilst everything from last season should still make you feel good, there may be one or two items you want to add or update.

Step Two: Moodboard

Imagine it's January 15, your mood is lower than the temperature, the sky is grey, and summer feels a long way off. The temptation to shove on old sweaters, crawl back under the duvet, and say "see you in spring!" is real. If you do not have a vision to work towards, it's even more tempting. Creating a seasonal style vision – one that aligns with your goals – helps you keep on track. It reminds you of what you're living (or dressing) up to, even when you want to go back to bed.

Step Three: Create outfits from what you already own

This helps you evolve your style without needing to buy anything new. You might discover new ways of wearing something; a pairing you didn't think of before. You may also find there are items you bought previously to fit some future ideal (as we discussed earlier) that now feel totally wearable. This is because you've evolved, so you're more comfortable being this version of yourself.

Give each outfit a rating out of 10 – for me, if it isn't an eight or above, then it's not added to my rotation, or it needs additional styling to make it pop.

You can also use the 10 Method to create outfits – not simply jeans and a nice top. Assign a number – 1 or 2, or 3 for really show-stopping items, including accessories. Now each outfit you create adds up to a 10. Let's say you're wearing jeans that are 2, a shirt that's a 1 – you have another 7 to find. You pull on your knee-high metallic boots (3) grab your fun, textured bag (2) then add a necklace. It's a 10.

Add these outfits to your digital wardrobe, so you're never in a "what should I wear today?" spin.

Step Four: Make a list of what you need

If you've got a functioning wardrobe that helps you feel your best, this list should generally be around five items max, and it's split into two categories:

1. The most-worn things. For winter, it might be a new pair of boots or a coat. These are the items that get worn every day throughout the season and come out on the other side with a cost-per-wear in the negative. For summer, it might be breezy dresses or sandals that took you from work to pub to weekend. Likely, given the usage, they look a little tired after a few months.
2. Updates to keep your style looking fresh. Whether there's a specific accessory everyone will be wearing this season – a scarf, a tie, brooches – put a bit of your budget towards these. Accessories are a great way of adding interest to your outfits, and showing you have fashion cred, without breaking the bank. Once you understand trends, you'll realise you don't have to go to what's new, either. Search for vintage, or visit artisan markets.

Step Five: Study shop

This is what stylists spend time doing, and it's why they get comments like, 'Are those the [Chanel boots]?' when they're actually wearing a similar-looking unlabelled vintage pair they found on eBay.

Now you understand the tiers of fashion, and how trends are created, you'll know to look out for what's upcoming – not right before the season starts, but a few months ahead. If you can get a feel for what everyone will be wearing, and incorporate a couple of the styles into your look now, you'll be seen as the one who goes first. And you'll pay less, because the eBay seller who's had the boots you want through an obsolescence will likely want to shift them now. When items are in demand, the price increases.

All this requires is an internet connection and maximum 20 minutes. Look up the runways and use your trends checklist to make a note of what looks fresh now.

Step Six: Don't shop by store, shop by item

We love familiarity, but it can breed contempt, or boredom. There will be certain stores that feel like home for you, but if they were satisfying every part of your style, you wouldn't be reading this.

Remember high street stores are taking inspiration from designer, street style, and vintage references. *Everything* in the store right now is a remake of something else. And that means you can probably find a better quality item elsewhere when you know exactly what you're looking for.

Those stores also use subtle tricks to get you to spend more – an additional bonus if you add another item you were never looking for to your cart, or a discount code for next time if you spend over a certain amount.

This is why you need a specific list of items you're looking for.

You can be so much more intentional and save time and money when you shop strategically, not emotionally. Avoid "I'll just see what's new in at…" late-night boredom scrolls. Delete the apps from your phone. It might sound harsh, but you're letting your feelings and laziness mess with your style again. If you've digitised your wardrobe, scroll through that instead and get renewed appreciation for what you already have.

If you don't know where to shop, grab a stack of magazines and make a note of the names of the stores where the things you like come from. Approach Instagram in a different way: do a deep-dive for independent brands – there are loads.

Go on to a marketplace, like Etsy, and search specific keywords. Set up your Google search with filters. If you type in "green skirt" you will be overwhelmed with results. If you type in "bottle green satin midi skirt, size [x]" and then filter results by price, store, and material, you will narrow down your options.

Step Seven: Add to your digital wardrobe *before* you buy

Once you've found your shortlist of items, add them to your digital wardrobe. Can you create at least five outfits using this item? Can you commit to wearing it at least 100 times? Does the quality seem like it will last that long? Try your best to be objective. Do you still want the item 24 hours later? If the answer to all the questions is yes, go ahead and add to the basket.

I know retailers want you to panic that it won't be available if you wait, but in my experience this is mostly untrue (didn't we cover this? After a lifetime of being marketed at on urgency, it bears repeating). Returns happen, items get restocked. Retailers have the technology to look at what's selling well, and what to order more of. If you're buying from an independent, message them directly and ask – mostly you'll find they are eager to help you, and will add you to the pre-order list for the next run.

Step Eight: Budget and return

Spend the most money on the things you will wear the most, and buy the best possible quality you can afford. Nine times out of 10, what you can afford is more than you think, because this process is about buying less, but spending more on individual items.

Buying online is convenient and can be fun, but it comes with the consequence of being a mindful consumer. Take your measurements before you shop and select the size for each individual item that best fits your size. Check the reviews as to whether this brand runs small or large.

For retailers that resell returns, there is roughly a 20 per cent refurbishment fee.[1] The increasing popularity of bracket buying (buying multiple sizes with the intention of returning whatever doesn't fit) and wardrobing (buying clothes, wearing them for an event, then returning them for a full discount) also leaves retailers with additional problems, and pushes the prices up for customers (though I'd like to note garment workers do not benefit from increased prices).

To be clear, I am not asking you to pity retailers; they have a responsibility to the environment and should improve their processes and sizing to ensure fewer returns. But buying mindfully means doing your research before you spend, so that in good faith and to the best of your knowledge, this item is going to add value to your wardrobe and become well-worn.

---

1. https://www.bbc.co.uk/worklife/article/20231004-why-more-fashion-retailers-are-charging-return-fees

Step Nine: Remember what style is

Style is not whatever our favourite store says it is, because we're too lazy to shop elsewhere. It's an eclectic mix of shapes, cuts, colours, accessories, and styles that someone would look at and think "so *you*." With this in mind, your fashion world becomes so much bigger. You're no longer consuming, you are creating.

Open your mind to new places to shop – smaller independents, vintage, second-hand, local retailers. Look for sources of inspiration that aren't the homepage of that particular store you find yourself constantly going back to, even though it's left you bored.

Chapter 25

The Outfit Diary

You're an expansive queen – look how far you've come!

It's always better to show, not tell. And that's why it's time for *The Outfit Diary: Round Two*. An opportunity for you to see how much you've evolved through this process and, of course (because we love an expansive queen) to see where you'd like to take things further still.

In having another go at this exercise, you'll see if and where you're still playing small, not being as daring as you could be, still underutilising your wardrobe, and talking yourself out of outfits and opportunities.

It was never a promise of this book to completely transform you. I am not a chrysalis. I am a woman who understands deeply all the reasons you've previously stood in front of your wardrobe and thought, 'I have nothing to wear. But I do hope that when you do this exercise for the second time, you will see how far you've come.

Here's how it works:

Every day for the next five days, take a photo of your outfit and answer the questions below.

- Today I am wearing…
- I decided to wear this because…

- What planning, prep or thought went into this outfit?
- On a scale of 1-10, with 1 being "a troll that lives under a bridge" and 10 being "a mediocre white man in middle management," how confident did you feel?
- Positive things that happened today…
- Negative things that happened today…
- How did the way you felt in your outfit impact your reaction(s) to these events?
- If I could improve this outfit in one way, what would it be?

Now take out your answers and images from when we did this exercise previously and put them side by side.

Ask yourself:

- What visual differences can I see?
- How has my style improved?
- In what ways have I grown in confidence?
- What would I like to improve my style still?
- **On a scale of 1-10 how would I rate my style now?**

Chapter 26

How to Use Your Wardrobe to Build Your Brand

Oh you know her – she's instantly recognisable and so freakin' stylish. She's everywhere, and she's fabulous.

Sprawled across the sofa, having finished what was reportedly a family-sized pudding, watching the *Great British Bake Off* and judging like I know anything about food (except how to eat it), my phone pinged. And then it pinged again.

Several messages through the course of the evening and next day, all saying a variation of the same thing: Have you seen this video? Is it about you?

A content creator had made a video sharing their opinion on the idea of getting dressed for work. When it comes to such matters, each to their own; we live in a democracy and my opinion carries no more weight or importance than anyone else's.

I do fear we've lost the art of discussion or debate; that we are pressured into taking a strong stance and sticking with it, even when new information comes to light. Nuance never existed in the online space when, ironically, nuance is all there is. You, your wardrobe, the things you believe or choose to see do not exist over *there*, or over *there* – they exist in the space between.

In this video, the person was sharing their opinion that what you wear doesn't matter. And in it, they referenced a specific item of jewellery. They referenced a Vivienne Westwood choker. Like the one I wear frequently. People sent me the video because they had made the association between the necklace, and me.

Let me tell you why I wear this necklace.

It's the story of me

When I was studying for my degree, I worked a few jobs to make ends meet, including in two hotels. Whilst my friends were going out or sleeping in, I was going to work. I lived in two parallel worlds in the same city. I heard the privileged conversations of privately-educated students, funded by their parents so they could spend their spare time theorising (and partying). And then amongst the hospitality workers, many of whom were also here to study, or send money back home to their families.

I didn't like the work at the hotels. It was physically demanding and there was a lot of pressure to turn rooms around as quickly as possible. But the people I worked with were wonderful and I learned a lot about the way the world works through conversations with them. We earned minimum wage, and we would usually have a minimum 11 rooms to clean per shift. If you had a day of only changeovers it was chaotic, and you'd generally only get through it on time because colleagues were kind enough to stay and help.

The hotels had regular guests because they were city-based and people were there for business. You learn a lot about human decency, respect, and class in a job like that. Because mostly, people look through you. Or pretend you aren't there. But one particular regular guest always made a point of speaking to us. She always left a generous tip, held the doors open, and said thank you. She left an expensive scent in the halls when she walked them, which I deduced from her room (I wanted to be a journalist, of course I'm nosy) was Armani Code. In her room were designer clothes, including Vivienne Westwood, and Vivienne Westwood jewellery.

I had long made vision boards with images from magazines torn out haphazardly and taped together, and watched films and TV shows with women whose style I admired. But this was the first time in real life I'd come into contact with someone whose life I coveted. And it wasn't about the trappings of success. Yes, the cared-for hair, perfume, and suits were aspirational, but many guests passed through the hotel with those things. It was her behaviour I admired most; that she had style and money and a busy career and she treated everyone, from me the housemaid to the manager, with the same level of respect. She saw me, the human, not me, the staff.

I made a promise with myself that I was working so hard now so that one day, I would have money and a successful career, and no matter what, I would never forget where I came from. I would treat everyone with the same level of respect, unless they proved themselves unworthy of respect (and that's never happened with a cleaning lady, funnily enough).

The Vivienne Westwood choker isn't just a pretty piece of jewellery or a way of showing off, and it certainly isn't a symbol to say "look how much better than you I am, I got dressed." It serves as a reminder to me, and symbolises what I stand for. It's the illustration of a story – and now I've told you this story, you'll remember it when you see the necklace.

That is how to use clothing for personal branding.

Who do you think of when you see that outfit?

At the mere mention of certain names, you think of certain outfits or items. Steve Jobs, whose style we earlier dissected, and his black turtleneck. Alex Hormozi and his vest and nose strips. Audrey Hepburn and the little black dress. Marilyn Monroe and the white halterneck. Carrie Bradshaw and her Manolos. Some of these were a moment-in-time that became lore. Others are staples. All of them were strategic choices – and repetition is key.

For one-time outfits that become part of culture, the repetition is in how many times you see it. For everything else, the repetition is in how many times it's worn. If you saw Steve Jobs in a turtleneck once, it would have no bearing on the image that came into your mind when you read his name. But seeing it over and over formed an association.

Clothing helps you tell a story. If you're starting out in business in a market everyone tells you is crowded, or you're making a name for yourself in your industry, you can use your wardrobe as a tool to get seen, known, and remembered.

You can also borrow the established brand of a clothing item to change your image. Which brands or items have the kind of perception you want to create for yourself?

Let's use Chanel as an example, because Coco was a master at crafting story through aesthetics. She understood that customers weren't buying a bag, they were buying status; a feeling, a symbol, a legacy. The interlocking C symbol is one of the most instantly-recognisable logos in the world. We all know what Chanel stands for, regardless of our interactions with, or relationship to, the brand. The enduring meaning of Chanel, which has long outlasted its founder, is testament to the commitment to a specific visual identity.

Certain quotes attributed to Chanel, like "a girl should be two things, classy and fabulous" and "dress shabbily and they remember the dress, dress impeccably and they remember the woman" mean that when you wear Chanel (or borrow the Chanel aesthetic), you are associated with those immortal words.

We wear our values

But a word of warning: when you stand for something and proudly inject that thing into your branding, customer loyalty relies on the maintenance of those values. If your values change or your perspective shifts, those customers will expect an explanation.

Chanel has come under fire in recent years for what shoppers consider to be a decline in quality. As we explored earlier, a decline across the board happened as fashion cycles sped up, social media changed the way we shop, and the economy fluctuated. But when your brand stands for timeless and enduring quality, you better make sure those factors don't impact your reputation.

The apparent decline in quality at Chanel has led to some critics and fashion content creators dubbing it "Zara for rich people."[1] Fashion and culture journalist Amy Odell asked the question: 'The Chanel brand has been confused for a while, maybe since Lagerfeld died in 2019. Does it want to be high-end Zara – or Hermès? Can it be both?'[2]

---

1. @allyshaps, Tiktok https://www.tiktok.com/@allyshaps/video/7378555579523960106
2. Odell, A. (2025) 'Will Chanel's weak results end bagflation?,' *Back Row*, 21

Writing in the *New York Times*, fashion editor and lecturer Katharine K. Zarrella said: 'Many luxury houses have broken the principles that made them so successful. These hoity-toity brands, which cheapened their essence and eviscerated their desirability with down-market celebrity partnerships, licensing deals and influencer advertising, have no one to blame but themselves.'

She suggested that brands like Chanel have cheapened themselves by going after the lower end of the market with diffusion and keyrings. 'We are mere minutes away from a Chanel- and Gucci-packed outlet store popping up in a midtier strip mall near you,' she added.

After the pandemic, these brands hiked their prices 'so the "wrong" people stop buying,' said Erez Yoeli, a research scientist at MIT's Sloan School of Management, in the same article. But part 'of the pressure in the marketplace comes from the fact that you do have to be legitimately better,' he said. 'And if you're not, you're going to suffer the consequences.'[3]

Just Get Dressed: End of chapter task

Branding is no longer simply for big brands; it's about the way you're perceived by your colleagues, customers, and the wider community. The compound effect of utilising your wardrobe on a daily basis to cement your brand story is what I call equity dressing. Most of this book has been dedicated to reducing your style tax and now that's done, it's time to build value.

May.   https://amyodell.substack.com/p/will-chanels-weak-results-end-bagfla tion.

3. Zarrella, K. (2024) 'Obscene Prices, Declining Quality: Luxury is in a death spiral,' *The New York Times*.

Which celebrities' style, TV show costumes, or characters stick in your mind and why?

Take one of them and break down each component of the visual strategy.

- Why do you think specific brand elements were chosen?
- Can you spot any patterns between the scenario in which they find themselves and the choice of outfit?
- Are there any patterns in the choice of hairstyle, makeup, and outfit?
- Is the look cohesive, or jarring, and why?

Now it's your turn. Use these questions to interrogate your own personal brand and start to build a coherent picture of how you'd like to be seen.

- If there was a phrase or slogan you'd like someone to think when they see you, what would it be? What does that phrase or slogan look like? Are there specific colours, styles, or items that you could use to say it without words?
- Do you have any stories attached to specific pieces of clothing that match your values, business, or aspirations? Write out those stories.
- Are there any brands that match the way you'd like to be perceived?
- If you were to look at your current personal brand in comparison to what you'd like it to be, what needs improvement?
- Pick out the key themes or things to repeat in your style that will create alignment between you and that brand's perceived value.

Just Get Dressed

- What is the hill you will die on, and what would you
  never compromise on in your style?
- What standards do you want to be known for, and are
  these truly reflected in your style?

This is the last exercise in the book, and it pulls together all the
work we've already done.

Conclusion
Just Get Dressed

This is what the future could look like for you: stylish, confident, and filled to the brim with the real you. No more hiding.

'Three people stopped me today to comment on my outfit,' she shouted excitedly as she came bounding up to me from across the street. For a second I didn't recognise her. She *looked* like a client, but she was… so much brighter.

At that moment, I was hit with the meaning of this work. She told me about how she'd doubled her income, and how she was having her home re-modelled, and how she was looking forward to her holiday. But the thing she kept talking about was how many other people had noticed the shift. Women she knew were using her change as a reason to do it themselves. Strangers were stopping her in the street.

And the thing she loved most was that her young children noticed the change. Mummy was more fun. They started wanting to experiment with their clothes, just like Mummy. She was showing them that being a woman, and a mother, does not mean self-sacrifice, and she was teaching them that size and age are to be celebrated, not something of which to feel ashamed.

This is not an isolated story. I've worked with hundreds of women personally and thousands by extension and every day I receive messages about how the work has transformed lives.

Just Get Dressed

Whether it's the big stuff, like speaking on stages or writing books, or the small stuff (which is actually the big stuff, because most of life is lived in everyday moments), like receiving a compliment on an outfit at the coffee shop, what you wear matters. It has a power that transcends the physical realm, but it doesn't start with the clothes.

It starts, as it has for every woman I've worked with no matter her salary or status, with the courageous decision to change.

An outfit doesn't feel like a particularly world-changing thing to create, but how we dress directly impacts what we do, and now more than ever society needs action-taking women.

During the Great Depression, sales of red lipstick went up. Then again, following 9/11 and the ensuing economic downturn, sales of cosmetics increased in the US by 11%. The Lipstick Index, a term reportedly coined by Estée Lauder, suggests that sales of lipstick are an indicator of economics.

The way we decorate ourselves physically has long been likened to armour. It's a way of steeling yourself in times of turmoil, boosting your confidence, and keeping calm and carrying on. Hitler notoriously despised makeup, specifically red lipstick, which he believed symbolised indulgence, foreign influence, and non-Aryan values. He reportedly banned women in the inner circle from wearing makeup or painting their nails.[1] American and UK-based manufacturers jumped on this during the Second World War, and brands created lipstick as a resistance, such as Elizabeth Arden's Victory Red. Given current events, it did not surprise me to find myself at the Charlotte Tilbury counter looking for a new red lipstick this week.

---

1. History Today (2013) 'Fashion and the Third Reich.'

Makeup or a good jacket may be futile in the face of impending doom, and they are certainly tools layered in privilege – but there is comfort and a sense of safety to be found in personal style during times of crisis. During the 2020-2021 years, dopamine dressing referred to our desire to put on all the outfits we'd been saving for special occasions and dancing around our kitchens. "Wearapy" is a fashion psychology term coined by Shakaila Forbes-Bell to describe "the practice of using clothes as a tool to help you either successfully navigate different emotional states, confront your feelings, honour or boost your mood."[2]

As Tamu Thomas, author of *Women Who Work Too Much* says, 'Expression is the antidote to oppression.' She suggested that rather than being caught up on algorithms, or what time to post, we imagine our content as cultural commentary; that if a digital archaeologist were to uncover this in hundreds of years, they would learn something about this specific moment in time. I view getting dressed in the same way. It's the marker of who you were at this specific moment in time, and a story about why.

What you wear is political. Whether because you are intentionally making a statement, or because the things you wear are the product of systems which rely on cheap labour, finite resources, and crafty psychological tactics which keep you in a "never enough" state of being. But on the days when political statement through style feels like an exhausting concept, don't underestimate the power of a good outfit for simply lifting your spirits.

It doesn't mean going out and buying new things (I would never advise that as a first step to anybody in a style rut). It means

---

2. Forbes-Bell, S. (2022) *Big dress energy: How Fashion Psychology Can Transform Your Wardrobe and Your Confidence*. Piatkus.

allowing yourself the small pleasure of wearing your favourite shoes, even if you're going nowhere but your desk. It's putting on the jewellery that's sitting in a box in the back of your wardrobe. It's applying perfume, and not saving it for the best. Who knows when best will come, if ever? One thing I do know is if today is the last day, you'll be glad you squeezed every bit of juice from life, from your wardrobe, and from your makeup drawer.

Us modern-day humans seem to believe that the markers of an important life are in great and major moments. Standing on stage, delivering the speech, winning the award. But when all is said and done, the things you'll cherish the most are the everyday moments. Holding hands with your partner, the smell of freshly baked bread, the sound of the rain as you go to sleep, grateful for shelter and warmth at a time when not everybody has those things.

An outfit or a slick of lipstick won't change the world, but they are a small way of dealing with what's going on in the world.

Whilst clothes are seen as frivolous and of little consequence, I hope the answer to "what are we wearing right now?" is: whatever brings us as much joy as possible.

As much as just getting dressed is a ritual, prayer or manifestation for yourself, it is other women's prayers answered, too. Women you will know closely and women you will never meet. Perhaps the woman sitting across from you in the coffee shop, hiding herself away in baggy black nothingness because she feels lost.

As I was writing this book in my local coffee shop, I caught a woman taking photos of me. When she realised I'd seen her, she said, 'I'm ever so sorry, I'm embarrassed, but I just think you look so good, I wanted to send a photo to my friend.'

And not too long after that, a woman wedged her trolley between me and the cheese (never a good idea) in the supermarket. 'I love your outfit!' she said, 'It's so refreshing when most people seem to be wearing their pyjamas!' The particular outfit in question was a burgundy blazer and jeans, hardly revolutionary and yet, in the age of homogenisation, a revolution.[3]

You will never have the opportunity to speak to every stranger you pass in the street. But you will have an opportunity to influence them with your outfit. The world is becoming less colourful.[4] You can choose to walk in a more joyful and colourful direction. You can choose the ultimate act of rebellion in a world relying on your submission: to be a woman who wears whatever the hell she wants.

Last year, I received a message from a woman who used to work in the same office as me. She was in another department and we never spoke – a failure on my part as much as anything. During the period in which we worked in the same place, I was carrying around all the baggage we've covered in this book.

In her message, she said that she had judged me as intimidating. She only realised when I shared my story online that I had struggled as much as she had, and that perhaps my apparent standoffishness was more about self-protection than being a bitch. She said seeing me share my story had encouraged her to not just work on the internal stuff, but on her style too. She had a

3. Directory, S. (2026) *What role does fast fashion play in cultural homogenization? →
Question.* https://fashion.sustainability-directory.com/question/what-role-does-fast-fashion-play-in-cultural-homogenization/.
4. Science Museum Group, 2020.

better job, a new location, and a wardrobe she loved. And as with all my clients in between then and now, her evolution was a knock-on effect of me making that courageous decision to work on mine.

Working on your personal style is not a selfish act. It has far-reaching consequences, many of which you will never know.

Whilst once a source of overwhelm and frustration, I hope that on our journey together we have transformed your wardrobe into a place of joy; somewhere you look forward to going each morning, and asking yourself: Who do I want to be today?

As Anne Klein once famously said: "Clothes won't change the world; the women who wear them will."

Each time you put on clothes, you're affirming your identity, creating your legacy, and shaping the world you want to live in.

There will be times in the future, long after you've read this book and tossed it onto a shelf that you feel lost, helpless, stressed, sad, angry, unwell, or overwhelmed. I hope you remember this one simple principle:

Just get dressed.

What to do next

Thank you for allowing me into your wardrobe. If you'd like to keep going with the work, visit www.justgetdressed.com where you'll find a free audio series, resources, and further support I've put together for you.

Epilogue: Audrey's Story

She could hear the sirens. Darkness. Across the city, giant lights searched the sky. She lit her candle and went back to her book.

Audrey was born in September, 1927. She was the eldest of five children and lived with her parents in Portsmouth. They were a working class family, and her dad worked in the dockyard – one of the biggest employers of the city at the time.

From an early age, Audrey had serious aptitude; she excelled at maths and English. Her parents could not afford much, but when she was 11, Audrey was awarded a scholarship to study at grammar school. At a meeting at the school, her mother wasn't sure it was a good idea, but the teacher was insistent due to Audrey's potential.

And then, days after her 12th birthday, Britain declared war. No grammar school for Audrey.

Audrey was a bookworm and she'd often be told off for reading with a candle under her bed when the air-raid sirens went off. Portsmouth was savaged in the war, thanks to the naval base. Her dad would tell stories about finding body parts in the wreckage.

The family lived in Amelia Street in central Portsmouth, an area for dockyard families, and their house got flattened in a strike which killed 18 people on December 23, 1940. By the grace of something unknown, the family were visiting an aunty in Clanfield, otherwise they could have been wiped out. They were relocated to Wymering, north Portsmouth.

Soon enough Audrey, along with her younger brothers and sister, was evacuated to the Isle of Wight, which is around five miles off mainland UK. She was told that under no circumstances should she allow her siblings to be separated.

The curse of the eldest daughter is that when she becomes a sibling, she becomes a stand-in parent. When Audrey and her siblings arrived on the Isle of Wight, residents came to collect evacuated children. But space for one or two children is *very* different to having space for five. Audrey refused to allow her siblings to be separated. Hours passed. It didn't look good.

Eventually, a kindly old man turned up at the station and agreed to take them all.

And after the war, aged 19, Audrey was back in Portsmouth working in a hospital, when she met a Glaswegian soldier named Jock (John). They married straight away and soon after had their first baby, one of seven. It was only on the maternity ward, when she was about to give birth, that Audrey learned from another mother where babies *actually* come from.

Audrey was having babies from age 19 to age 40.

Jock was arguably not a good husband (though he was reportedly a better father); he was often away for work, in scrapes with the police, sometimes in prison, and the host of big parties for the entire estate, on which he'd spend most of the family's money. He was reportedly on the front of the national papers when he got sent down for affray. One of their children, Kathy, had cerebral palsy, and passed away aged 16. Despite their hardships, and what must have been deep-seated trauma from the circumstances of their lives, they loved each other fiercely.

Audrey was a hard worker, taking on all sorts of jobs during her younger years in between children. She had a tough shell and a soft interior, though she was not a particularly maternal figure, which perhaps makes sense since she became a stand-in parent as a wartime child. Her younger brother Lenny lived with her and Jock for a long time, and even though his name was often mud, she made sure to look after Len. She could talk shit about Lenny all day long; if anyone else tried it, they'd be in trouble. Except on Saturdays after she'd been into the spirits, when she'd chuck him out and he'd walk past the house sticking up his middle fingers shouting expletives.

Whilst she could be considered flawed, as all humans are, in glamour, Audrey was other-worldly. She had "it" – a *je ne sais quoi*. That mysterious way of looking effortlessly stylish (though I suspect it secretly took a lot of effort). Pictures of her from the 1960s show her wearing fur coats and lipstick. And she would not be seen dead outside without perfectly coiffed hair, soaked in perfume to hide the stale cigarette smoke. She used to let one of her granddaughters brush and style her hair when she was little. Audrey would not set foot out of the door with unbrushed hair. Even in her later years, she would take her time getting ready for a trip to the supermarket, always in a blazer and large sunglasses. She was an early adopter of the Ugg boot and loved a neck scarf.

Audrey died relatively penniless, a serial chainsmoker and frequent drinker, in a small council home over the road from the one she grew up in, and five doors down from the one in which she raised her family.

In life, she was intelligent, bold, sassy, sometimes angry, passionate, emotional, hypocritical, sometimes chaotic, funny, often drunk, and objectively striking. She had auburn hair that matched her personality – so bright and rich, it burned like the candles she used to read her books by. But she never got to fulfil her potential.

And whilst her story is not a sad one – how can a life filled with love be called anything other than a triumph? – what might she have become, achieved, or created had she been able to go to grammar school? What might she have done if she were in her youth today, with the tools available to us? What schemes, dreams, and goals could she have achieved with a mobile phone in her hand? What could she have done with a wifi connection and half-decent coffee?

Audrey was my grandmother. I'm the one who used to love brushing her hair. And she is the reason I wrote this book.

I can still hear her raspy laugh, smell her perfume, taste the "meals" she used to make us (ice cream soda and Jaffa Cakes; she was not the best chef). I still laugh sometimes at how she would see us coming up the road, and (having been told off endlessly for smoking) could be seen through the lace curtains going, 'shit shit shit', spraying air freshener all around the room, making it worse.

Audrey is the person I think of when I am procrastinating over writing this book. When the bigness of the concepts I unfurl in these pages feel too much. When I imagine the first shitty Amazon review, or the people just waiting for me to fuck it up.

She risked her life to read books; the least I can do is write one.

I think about her when I get dressed in the morning. I remember how she always – *always* – put herself together. She used clothes as armour, branding, and comfort. I remember her now through clothes, and that is their enduring power. Every time I put on a navy blazer, or a big pair of sunglasses, I am channeling my inner Audrey. Because right up until the end, she just got dressed.

The challenges, tasks and words on these pages are for every woman here now and in the future, who needs a regular reminder of who the fuck she is.

And they're also for the women before us, who never got the opportunity to find out.

www.ingramcontent.com/pod-product-compliance
Lightning Source LLC
Chambersburg PA
CBHW020316160726
47992CB00004B/1561